PREPARE

WORKBOOK WITH DIGITAL PACK

B1

LEVEL 4

Gareth Jones   Second Edition

Cambridge University Press
www.cambridge.org/elt

Cambridge Assessment English
www.cambridgeenglish.org

Information on this title: www.cambridge.org/9781009022965

© Cambridge University Press and Cambridge Assessment 2015, 2019, 2021

First published 2015
Second Edition 2019
Second Edition update 2021

20 19 18 17 16

Printed in Malaysia by Vivar Printing

A catalogue record for this publication is available from the British Library

ISBN 978-1-009-02296-5 Workbook with Digital Pack
ISBN 978-1-009-02295-8 Student's Book with eBook
ISBN 978-1-009-02297-2 Teacher's Book with Digital Pack

CONTENTS

ALL ABOUT ME

Describing people

1 Find and circle the adjectives for describing people.

weightpolitecarelesstownfunnybookfriendlymiserableconfidentbuycarefulcheerfulrudecarseriousrunshyunfriendlyfriday

2 Write the correct adjective.

1 Mark never knows where things are – he loses most of them. c_____

2 The woman in the shop said some horrible things. r_____

3 What a lovely girl! She's always smiling and so pleasant. c_____

4 Peter's older brother isn't very nice to us when we go to his house. u_____

5 Carly never talks to people she doesn't know at parties. s_____

6 Emma feels very unhappy because she doesn't like her new school. m_____

7 Mum likes you because you say 'please' and 'thank you'! p_____

8 When I study, I concentrate so I don't make mistakes. c_____

3 Choose the correct answer in each sentence.

1 Sarah is always making people laugh. She's really _____.
  a serious **b** funny **c** unfriendly

2 Lots of people like my dad. He is very _____.
  a friendly **b** shy **c** careful

3 In class, Louisa is _____. She answers all the questions the teacher asks her.
  a rude **b** confident **c** miserable

4 Ben doesn't like making mistakes. He's very _____.
  a careless **b** careful **c** polite

5 He never smiles. I think he's a bit too _____.
  a shy **b** cheerful **c** serious

4 Look at the pictures and choose the correct word to complete the description. You can only use each word once.

attractive	bald	blonde	dark	curly
early twenties	elderly	fair	good-looking
handsome	late thirties	middle-aged
pretty	straight	teenage

a Sara is in her [1]_____. She has long dark [2]_____ hair. She's an [3]_____ woman.

b John has curly hair and is [4]_____ and [5]_____.

c Anne is [6]_____. She has got short straight hair.

d Freddie has got short [7]_____ hair. He's [8]_____.

e Stefanie is very [9]_____. She has [10]_____ hair and is in her [11]_____.

f Nicky is a [12]_____ girl. She's got long [13]_____ hair, which is [14]_____.

g Bobbie is in his fifties and is [15]_____.

1 Read this text about birth order quickly. Complete headings A–D with the words in the box.

> Eldest child   Middle child
> Only child   Youngest child

BIRTH ORDER

Some people believe your position in your family can change the kind of person you are. Which one are you?

A ....

You are very careful because you want to do everything right. You were first, so you are the example! You enjoy doing **(1)** .... homework, making lists and planning. You **(2)** .... like anything unexpected to happen.

B ....

You consider other people's feelings and hate it when people don't agree. You want **(3)** .... to be happy. You're friends **(4)** .... all your brothers' and sisters' friends. You can be really funny, too.

C ....

You never do anything wrong! You are **(5)** .... baby of the family, and everyone loves you! You want everyone to watch you. You like people and people like you! Oh, and you really enjoy having surprises!

D ....

You prefer being with adults, not children your own age. You're good **(6)** .... everything you do. You love reading and have a clear view of the world. You hate it when you don't succeed.

2 Read the text again. For questions 1–6 think of the word which best fits each gap. Use only one word in each gap.

3 Which 'child' do you think wrote these comments?

1 ....
I'm just like that. I hate birthdays for that reason – you never know if someone is going to suddenly do something that you didn't know about. I hate that.
Judith, Indonesia

2 ....
I don't know. I mean, I haven't got any brothers or sisters, but I've got a lot of cousins. I don't think that these things are always correct. I don't think they're true!
Cim, Turkey

3 ....
This one is sort of right – I mean, I have got a lot of friends, and people laugh with me at my jokes. But I don't really mind if people are unhappy – you can't be happy all the time!
Zé Miguel, Portugal

4 ....
I hate it when they say things like this! It's just not true! I'm not a baby! Grrrr!
Nini, Peru

4 Match the highlighted words in the text to their meanings.

1 certain or obvious ....
2 events that you didn't expect to happen ....
3 think carefully about something ....
4 organising something for the future ....

GRAMMAR Present simple and continuous

1 Complete the sentences with the correct form of the verbs in brackets.

1 Julia _____ every day at 7 am. (get up)
2 Tonight, my parents _____ a TV show on their computer. (watch)
3 Martin _____ his new trainers. They're really nice! (wear)
4 We _____ our homework in our rooms. (finish)
5 Every day my dad _____ 5 km before work. (run)

2 Choose the correct verb forms.

1 I *am hating / hate* it when my bedroom isn't tidy.
2 I *don't believe / am not believing* that robots can do things better than humans.
3 I *am having / have* my birthday party at my favourite restaurant.
4 One day I *want / am wanting* to go to Australia.
5 I *am sending / send* you this email to give you the flight information.
6 I *don't understand / am not understanding* what you mean.
7 My mother *is owning / owns* a computer company.
8 I really *am liking / like* making pizza.

3 Complete the sentences with the words in the box.

always	every year	later today	never
next month	right now	sometimes
this term	tomorrow	tonight

1 _____ my birthday is on a different day!
2 We're learning about plant life in biology _____.
3 _____ we're spending two weeks by the sea – it's holiday time!
4 I can't go to the cinema tonight because we're visiting my aunt in hospital _____.
5 My music teacher's classes are _____ a lot of fun!
6 _____ I'm going to a party at my friend's house!
7 I _____ go to bed before 8.30 pm.
8 I have an exam _____, so I'm going to bed early tonight.
9 My sister _____ goes running before school. Other times she stays in bed!
10 I'll speak to you later because I'm tired _____.

4 Correct the mistakes in these sentences, or tick (✓) any you think are correct.

1 When we are together, we are having fun.
2 I write to tell you that I have a new computer.
3 I send you this email to invite you to my birthday party on Saturday.
4 We go out together every week.

VOCABULARY Prefixes: *un-*, *in-*, *im-*

1 Write the opposite of the adjectives in the correct column.

correct	expensive	fair	friendly
healthy	kind	known	lucky
patient	polite	visible	well

un-	in-	im-

2 Match the comments 1–6 with words from Exercise 1.

1 I have enough money to buy it because it's so cheap. _____
2 Our team played better than the other team but didn't win. _____
3 She always wants everything done immediately. _____
4 He's never nice to me when I see him at school. _____
5 Smoking is very bad for you. _____
6 The bus driver never says 'hello' or 'goodbye'. _____

3 Use words from Exercise 1 to complete the sentences.

1 a Sabrina's not going to school because she's sick.
 b Yes, she looks very _____.
2 a Look at the fog – I can't see anything!
 b Yes, the house right opposite is almost _____!
3 a He always says bad things about people.
 b I know, I think he's really _____.
4 a The doctor was wrong when he told me to stop working.
 b Do you think his advice was _____?
5 a Carl cheats when we play computer games and he always wins.
 b That's really _____!
6 a Do you think there's life on other planets?
 b That's something _____.

WRITING An online profile

1 Before you read the two online profiles, tick (✓) the information you think people will include.

1 an online username ☐
2 a description of what they look like ☐
3 where they live ☐

4 a description of their personality ☐
5 friends' hobbies ☐

FaceNet

 👤 **Profile** ⚙ **Account**

Ritzy_2006

My name's Rita, but my friends call me Ritzy. My hair is short, dark and curly! I'm from Canada and I live in the capital – Ottawa. I go to Williamson High School and my favourite subject is maths. I like to say what I think, but sometimes people say I'm a bit impolite. I get good marks at school and my teachers say I'm quite intelligent, so I am doing something right! I'm really into sports, and I play tennis well. I'm also learning the guitar at the moment. I don't have my own guitar, but I have asked my parents to get me one for my birthday!

Start 1

Hey guys, I'm Sam! My hair is short, dark and curly. I'm from South Africa, but I live in New York. My hobbies are watching movies and acting – I'm hoping to be famous one day! I go to drama classes two times a week, which is very important because I want to be an actor. I'm a friendly person and I'm fairly confident, but I can be quite impatient and sometimes people think I'm a bit unfair! I don't do much exercise, so I sometimes feel a bit unhealthy!

2 Read the two online profiles. Decide who does the following things. Write *Sam* or *Rita*.

1 _____ lives in a different place from where he / she was born.
2 _____ has one subject he / she really likes at school.

3 _____ has classes outside school.
4 _____ does an outdoor activity.
5 _____ wants to be a star.
6 _____ is from North America.

3 Add the missing vowels (a, e, i, o, u) to make adverbs.

1 __ b __ t
2 q __ __ t __

3 r __ __ l l y
4 v __ r y

5 f __ __ r l y

4 Write some information about yourself for these notes.

What's your name?

Which country do you come from?

Where do you live?

What do you look like?

What type of person are you?

What is your favourite subject at school?

What are your hobbies and interests?

5 Write an online profile about yourself.

- Use the tips in the *Prepare to write* box, Student's Book, page 13.
- Use adverbs to make adjectives stronger or weaker.
- Remember to check your spelling and grammar.
- Write about 100 words.

2 IN FASHION

VOCABULARY Clothes: adjectives

1 Write the letters in the correct order to make adjectives.

1 adlyb-edressd ....
2 dnsceo-dhna ....
3 ufnhensoalabi ....

4 acusla ....
5 uclfbntaremoo ....

2 Match the words to their meanings.

1 loose-fitting ....
2 comfortable ....
3 smart ....
4 skinny ....
5 brand new ....
6 trendy ....
7 well-dressed ....

a narrow and fitting closely to the body
b wearing attractive, good-quality clothes
c large and comfortable to wear
d gives a pleasant feeling
e having a clean, tidy and stylish appearance
f completely new
g popular at a particular time

3 Complete the sentences with the correct word from Exercise 1

1 I don't like these trainers. They are very trendy, but they are really ....
2 I always buy .... clothes because they're so cheap!
3 My clothes looked great five years ago. Now they look so ....
4 My dad never wears nice clothes. He's really .... !
5 It's only a small party at a friend's house. I'm going to wear .... clothes.

4 Complete the conversation with words from Exercises 1 and 2.

1 **A:** Are you wearing your .... jeans to the concert?
   B: Yes, I am. But they are a bit ....
2 **A:** Is that a .... jacket?
   B: No, it's .... , from the new sports shop in town.
3 **A:** She is so .... and always wears the latest fashions!
   B: Yes, she isn't the type of person to be .... !
4 **A:** The restaurant sign says .... clothes only.
   B: I'm going home to change these old clothes because I am so ....
5 **A:** Sam doesn't worry about how he looks. He prefers a .... style!
   B: He's not like his brother, who is really .... He wears the best clothes.

1 Look at the article about shoes before reading it. Tick (✓) where it comes from.

  1 a blog ☐   **2** an email ☐   **3** a teen magazine ☐   **4** an online forum ☐

2 Read the article. Are these sentences true (T) or false (F)?

  1 Many readers buy expensive shoes. ....

  2 At Raffi's school, everyone wears the same colour trousers/skirt. ....

  3 Raffi wears the same shoes as his friends. ....

  4 Anne Belle wrote her name on her trainers. ....

  5 At Zehra's school, her classmates wear stylish shoes. ....

  6 Zehra admires her art teacher's style. ....

3 Match the highlighted words in the article to their meanings.

  1 protect ....   **a** things that you say or write that express your opinion

  2 comments ....   **b** a group of things or people

  3 collection ....   **c** very important and necessary

  4 essential ....   **d** keep someone or something safe from something dangerous or bad

4 Complete the sentences with a word from Exercise 3.

  1 He always wears sunglasses to .... his eyes from the sun.

  2 Jane likes to write .... on social media about the clothes people wear in their photos.

  3 Some people think it's .... to look trendy all the time.

  4 I love the new fashion .... at G&C this summer.

What do you think about SHOES?

We all wear shoes every day. They **protect** our feet from the things we do every day – walking, school activities, sports and so on. But for some people they are more than that. They follow shoe styles, and a good pair of trendy shoes or trainers will not be cheap. *Mag About You* did a survey and we discovered that many of you pay a lot of money for shoes. We think it's because they are an **essential** fashion item – specially for the youth of today! A pair of shoes can make or break your style!

Here are some of the **comments** from the survey.

I think it's a bit boring the way everyone in my school wears the same black leather shoes. There are all kinds of shoes we could wear, but we have a uniform, and most people follow the rules. There is one girl in my class who wears all kinds of different things and she's creative, but she isn't fashionable in my opinion. My friends and I try to be a bit different and wear black trainers instead. We buy them from the same shop, but we like them!

👤 *Raffi, South Africa*

I love shoes, especially trainers. They are trendy and comfortable. You can wear them with everything – trousers, skirts and so on. At school we did a project where we had to add something to a pair of white trainers. I wrote half my name on the left and the other half on the right. It was such a cool project!

👤 *Anne Belle, New Zealand*

At my school we all have to wear these silly black or brown shoes. They look quite scruffy after a few months. Nobody likes them. Anyway, the kinds of shoes we can wear at school is a big story at the moment! The school agrees now that the style of the uniform is unfashionable. Our art teacher can give the school some advice! She has a great **collection** of shoes, and in the summer her sandals are always so pretty. She's really well-dressed. I want to dress like her.

👤 *Zehra, Turkey*

Next week: What do you think about school bags?
Click here to answer our questions.

GRAMMAR   Past simple

1 Complete the sentences with the verbs in brackets in the past simple.

1 Yesterday I _____ my new jacket to school. (wear)
2 After watching Rihanna's new video, everyone _____ a trendy T-shirt like hers. (want)
3 Mum _____ to take her shoes back to the shop. (forget)
4 Dad _____ into town to get Mum a new pair of earrings. (go)
5 Lots of my friends _____ their new Nike trainers online. (buy)
6 Emily _____ the fashion show in London last week. (enjoy)
7 _____ you text Mac about the sale in Zara next week? (do)
8 Serena _____ really smart in her new dress on Friday. (look)
9 Andrew _____ a new suit and tie for his birthday. (get)
10 My brother _____ wearing caps when he was younger. (love)

2 Write the questions for these answers.

1 what / you / do?

_____

I went clothes shopping with my friend.

2 your dad / buy / a new shirt?

_____

No, he didn't. He bought a pair of shoes instead.

3 go / cinema / with / parents?

_____

No, I visited my friends instead.

4 do / wear / new jumper?

_____

I did! Everyone loved it!

5 how long / film / last?

_____

About two hours, I think.

6 eat / restaurant / after the fashion show?

_____

Yes, we did. We had burgers and salad.

7 you / get home / late?

_____

No, we didn't. I think we got home at 8.30 pm.

8 your parents / buy / new skirt?

_____

Yes, they gave me the money and I got it from Kool Klothez.

9 What / you / get / birthday?

_____

I got some new trainers and a T-shirt.

3 Complete the sentences. Put the verbs into the correct positive or negative form.

1 It was raining, so I _____ my umbrella. (take)
2 The book was boring and I _____ it at all. (enjoy)
3 We _____ to Spain for our holidays from Heathrow Airport. (fly)
4 My best friend _____ me a lovely birthday present. (give)
5 Suni _____ to play with Marta because he was watching TV. (want)
6 It was a hot day and we _____ lots of water. (drink)
7 You _____ me last week because you had to do your homework. Remember? (visit)
8 She _____ you an email this morning. (send)

4 Complete the text with the verbs in the box. Use the past simple, positive or negative.

ask	buy	catch	go	look
see	smile	spend	tell	visit

Eve [1] _____ shopping with her parents in London last week. They [2] _____ a train from Bristol to London. They [3] _____ two days there. They [4] _____ all the best shops for clothes in the main shopping areas like Oxford Street, Camden and Carnaby Street! Eve is so lucky because her mum [5] _____ her what type of clothes she wanted. So she [6] _____ her a lot of trendy things like skinny jeans and cool white trainers. She was wearing them when I [7] _____ her at the party on Friday. She [8] _____ so happy when people [9] _____ her how nice her clothes were – she [10] _____ all night long. I think I need to go to London soon, too!

5 Choose the correct sentence in each pair.

1 a We were there for three days because last week is a holiday.
   b We were there for three days because last week was a holiday.
2 a Last Saturday I went to the cinema with my friends.
   b Last Saturday I go to the cinema with my friends.
3 a The National Park is a clean and quiet place, so we chose to go there.
   b The National Park is a clean and quiet place, so we choosed to go there.
4 a She so surprised and really happy!
   b She was so surprised and really happy!
5 a I have a lot of fun last weekend.
   b I had a lot of fun last weekend.

1 Write the letters in the correct order to make adverbs.

1 dalby ....
2 larceufly ....
3 yarley ....
4 saft ....
5 ellw ....
6 halilhtey ....
7 vaheyli ....
8 lraey ....

2 Complete the sentences with adverbs from Exercise 1.

1 I always go to bed .... before an exam.
2 Eating .... makes me feel better.
3 It's raining ...., so I'll stay at home today.
4 You're driving too ....! Slow down!
5 Georgina looks really .... after going to the gym.
6 Paul visits his family in South Africa ...., usually in August.
7 My team played .... this year.
8 Jamie thinks .... before he speaks.

1 Look at the photo. Where are the teens? Tick (✓) the event where you think they are.

1 a special birthday party ☐
2 a party at the end of high school ☐
3 a wedding party ☐

🔊 **01 2** Now listen and check your answer.

🔊 **01 3** Listen again and choose the correct answers.

1 Rob is talking about his *cousin / sister*, Denise.
2 Denise left school *last year / two years ago*.
3 Rob thinks proms are *British / American*.
4 Rob thinks it *is / isn't* a good idea to spend a lot of money on a prom dress.
5 Denise got a job in a *café / clothes shop*.
6 Lara says she is *going to / not going to* buy her prom dress herself.

🔊 **01 4** Listen again and complete the first part of the conversation.

Lara: Hey, Rob, is that your sister? She's ¹ ....!
Rob: Yeah, that's Denise! And that's a ² .... from last year! Do you ³ .... Lara? She went to that end-of-year ⁴ ...., the prom.
Lara: Yes. And is that Andy Patterson with her? He's very ⁵ ...., isn't he?
Rob: Yep! In his ⁶ .... tie!
Lara: I can't ⁷ .... till our prom, can you?
Rob: Do you think I'm going to wear a tie like that?
Lara: Yes, you have to! Everyone does when they ⁸ .... school.
Rob: Hmm. I think the prom comes from ⁹ .... I don't like it.

VOCABULARY Life events

1 Add the missing vowels (a, e, i, o, u) to complete these life events.

1 b__ b__rn
2 g__t __ d__gr____
3 g__t __ dr__v__ng l__c__nc__
4 g__t __ j__b
5 h__v__ ch__ldr__n
6 r__t__r__
7 l____v__ h__m__

8 st__rt sch____l
9 g__t m__rr____d
10 g__ t__ __n__v__rs__ty
11 l____v__ sch____l
12 m__v__ h__m__
13 v__t__

2 Look at the pictures. What are they celebrating? Write a life event from Exercise 1 in each space.

1 _____ 2 _____ 3 _____ 4 _____ 5 _____

3 Complete the sentences with the correct form of the words from Exercise 1.

1 I want to _____ in London and study history.
2 I _____ for my local politician last week.
3 My dad _____ in the last century.
4 I've just _____ because I like this house more than my last one.
5 In my country, all children _____ when they are between 16 and 18.
6 I want to _____ and then buy a second-hand car.
7 My sister _____ after working at the bookshop for 50 years.
8 My friend's older brother _____ as a car mechanic.

4 Match the questions and the answers.

1 What is Charlie going to study at university? _____
2 When were you born? _____
3 When did you start school? _____
4 Do you think you will have children? _____
5 Is your sister going to leave school next year? _____
6 Why are you moving home? _____
7 When do you think you will retire? _____
8 When did you first vote? _____

a Definitely not before I am 30!
b On 30th May 2006.
c He wants to get a degree in English.
d We need more space for the baby.
e I don't think so, and anyway she's only 16.
f I went to school when I was six years old.
g Probably when I am 70!
h In the general election just after my 18th birthday.

READING

1 Read the title of the newspaper article. Tick (✓) the information you think it will include. Read the article quickly and check.

1 not much choice in courses ☐
2 the number of students who dislike school ☐
3 reasons students are unhappy at school ☐
4 the most boring subjects at school ☐
5 the best types of jobs ☐
6 a solution to the problem ☐

EDUCATION IS BORING
AND DOESN'T PREPARE THEM FOR
THE FUTURE,
SAY STUDENTS

Do you find your school lessons boring? Many teenagers say they don't enjoy their classes and think the education system needs to change to make it more interesting and useful.

Around 80% of students said they were unhappy with their school life, and almost 50% said there were not enough courses to choose from.

When asked how they felt about their education, students said they often didn't find it very interesting. 'It does only a tiny bit to help us find employment,' says Naomi, 16, from Cardiff. 'This really needs to change so our education makes sure we are helped to become successful later in life.'

Nicholas, 13, from London says when he is studying in class, he is often exhausted because he is always doing tests, which makes him lose interest. 'It's always about getting good results in tests, not about giving you more knowledge to help you when you leave school to get a job.'

The other thing students say is a problem is that often the lessons don't include anything connected to their interests. 'They don't seem to know who we are as young people in the 21st century. There isn't much technology used in the classroom, whereas in our personal lives, we – and everyone else – use technology in lots of different and exciting ways,' says Jessie, 16, from Winchester.

Education experts agree: 'Today's system is too focused on helping students pass exams and it doesn't help them prepare themselves for real life and work,' says Nigel Jones from EducateUK, an organisation that wants to make changes to the education system.

But what can be done to change this? 'We need to focus education on helping young people to develop the skills and knowledge they need in the modern world,' says Jones. 'We think that there should be a new, more relaxed course system that gives teachers more choices to make lessons more fun, interesting and practical.'

The idea is popular with students too. 'I'd love to have new, more useful classes at my school,' says Mark, 14. 'I'd like to learn computer programming so that I can become a video-games developer when I'm older.'

2 Read the newspaper article and answer the questions.

1 Most students say that they think their education is
   a good enough.
   b not good enough.
2 Naomi thinks that the education system
   a isn't very good at helping students find a job.
   b helps students be successful in life.
3 Nicholas says he feels tired because he
   a has a job after school.
   b does lots of exams.
4 Jessie thinks that teachers
   a don't use technology enough in the classroom.
   b use technology too much in the classroom.
5 Nigel Jones thinks education
   a needs to change.
   b should prepare students for exams.
6 Nigel thinks that lessons should be
   a more relaxing.
   b more useful.

3 Match the highlighted words in the article to their meanings.

1 _____ giving most attention to
2 _____ facts and information
3 _____ things you can do well
4 _____ work
5 _____ useful in real situations

4 Complete the sentences with a word from Exercise 3.

1 It can be difficult to find _____ after leaving school.
2 I want to get a really good job where I can use my _____.
3 This book has some really _____ tips on how to pass English exams.
4 My uncle has a very good _____ of trains.
5 My sister is in her last year of high school and is really _____ getting into a good university.

1 Write the comparative and superlative forms of the following adjectives.

Adjective	Comparative	Superlative
1 big		
2 great		
3 safe		
4 easy		
5 exciting		
6 good		
7 bad		

2 Choose the correct words to complete the dialogue.

A: Hi, Rob. How are you?
B: Great, thanks! I'm going to see the [1]*latest / later* Star Wars movie.
A: Sounds amazing! Where are you going to watch it?
B: At the Globe Cinema. It's the [2]*best / bestest* in the city.
A: What time of day can you get the [3]*cheapest / most cheap* tickets?
B: At 2 p.m.
A: What are the snacks like there?
B: Oh! They have the [4]*tastier / tastiest* hot dogs!
A: Do you think this Star Wars film is going to be the [5]*more scary / most scary*?
B: I don't know, but maybe it's going to be the [6]*amazingest / most amazing*!

3 Complete the sentences with the correct form of the adjectives in brackets.

1 Simon is _____ person in our class. (popular)
2 Are people who live in Edinburgh _____ than people who live in London? (happy)
3 Where is _____ street in the world? (short)
4 Singapore is _____ to live in than St Petersburg. (expensive)
5 In the USA the age at which people can drive a car is _____ than in the UK. (young)

4 Write the words in the correct order to make sentences.

1 Valentina's university / as / isn't / Charly's / modern / as

2 Your city / as / isn't / Marco's / as / big

3 I don't have / apps / many / as / my / as / friend

4 Zoe / as / as / tall / Louis / isn't

5 People say that New York / dangerous / isn't / New Orleans / as / as

6 Here in the countryside, / as / as / fast / in / the internet speed isn't / city / the

5 Write the sentences using *not as ... as*.

1 Running is faster than swimming.

2 Mexico is hotter than Germany.

3 Antonia is friendlier than her sister.

4 Playing sports is healthier than playing video games.

5 Cats are more intelligent than dogs.

6 The maths exam was harder than the science exam.

6 Correct the mistakes and write new sentences or tick (✓) any you think are correct.

1 My sister older invited her to go out with us.

2 My grandad became more happy.

3 We go horse riding together, but I am not more good than her.

4 He's a bit tallest and thinerer than me.

5 We saw the laterest film with Tom Hiddleston. I liked it!

1 Rewrite the sentences so that they mean the same. Use *too*, *enough* or *not enough*.

1 This phone is too small.

2 This jacket isn't loose enough.

3 We have lots of space for the baby.

4 This computer is too slow.

5 My mum's car isn't big enough for our bikes.

6 We have lots of players in the team.

2 Complete the text with *too* or *enough*.

Yesterday I wanted to go into town. It was [1]_____ far to walk, and so I decided to get the bus. When the bus arrived, there wasn't [2]_____ room for me because it was [3]_____ crowded. The bus wasn't big [4]_____! So finally I walked into town.

>> See *Prepare to write* box, Student's Book, page 23.

1 Look at the picture. What is happening?

2 Read this email from your English-speaking friend Andy to see if you're right.

Fun!

Tell Andy

Yes – say how

Suggest ...

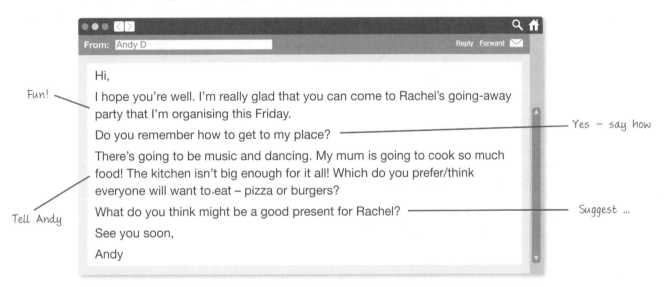

Hi,

I hope you're well. I'm really glad that you can come to Rachel's going-away party that I'm organising this Friday.

Do you remember how to get to my place?

There's going to be music and dancing. My mum is going to cook so much food! The kitchen isn't big enough for it all! Which do you prefer/think everyone will want to eat – pizza or burgers?

What do you think might be a good present for Rachel?

See you soon,

Andy

3 In informal emails, it's important to use short forms. Rewrite these sentences using short forms.

1 He has not got his phone with him.

2 She does not know anyone here.

3 We are going to leave soon.

4 I am bored.

5 What is your friend's name?

4 Plan an email to Andy, giving him your answers to his questions. Write down your ideas using the following responses.

You think the party will be fun.

Give the directions to Andy's place.

Say which food you prefer and why.

Suggest a good present for Rachel.

5 Write your email to Andy, using all the notes.

- Write about 100 words.
- Remember to check your spelling and grammar.
- Remember to use informal words and expressions, and short forms.

4 CHAMPIONS

VOCABULARY Sports

1 Find 12 sports words in the word square (→ ↓).

x	v	o	l	l	e	y	b	a	l	l
w	m	a	t	h	l	e	t	i	c	s
d	h	s	u	r	f	i	n	g	s	g
w	i	n	d	s	u	r	f	i	n	g
u	s	w	i	m	m	i	n	g	r	a
r	c	l	i	m	b	i	n	g	u	b
j	o	g	g	i	n	g	m	k	g	o
i	t	e	n	n	i	s	i	q	b	x
f	t	e	l	h	n	w	u	a	y	i
g	y	m	n	a	s	t	i	c	s	n
w	p	t	e	c	y	c	l	i	n	g

2 Complete the table with the sports from Exercise 1. Some may go into more than one category.

In/on water	Usually indoors	Usually outdoors

3 Complete the sentences with the correct form of the verb: *go*, *play* or *do*.

1 Let's _____ snowboarding in the mountains at the weekend!
2 My little sister _____ gymnastics every Saturday morning – she's getting really good!
3 I can't wait to _____ surfing at the weekend.
4 Elise wants to _____ ice skating with us.
5 My dad loves watching his favourite team _____ rugby.
6 My older brother _____ climbing in his free time.
7 I want to be a professional, so I _____ tennis as much as I can.
8 Do you want to _____ basketball after school?
9 I might _____ swimming on Saturday. Do you want to come?
10 John _____ jogging around the park for an hour a day.
11 My friend _____ ice hockey at the sports centre on Wednesdays.
12 Would you like to _____ table tennis with us?
13 It rained, and so we didn't _____ athletics.
14 We _____ volleyball in the sports hall at school.
15 When the weather is nice, I often _____ windsurfing on the lake.
16 I get really fit when I _____ squash.

The amazing health benefits of snowboarding

1 You are going to read an article about the benefits of snowboarding. Read the article quickly and tick (✓) the best alternative title.

1 How to stay healthy in your teens ☐
2 Snowboarding has great benefits for teens ☐
3 Snowboarding help teens stay out of trouble ☐

Snowboarding is an exciting outdoor activity and is becoming very popular among teenagers. Here, we find out how it can help you to become more healthy and enjoy life more.

Taking chances is a great way to help you to have confidence in yourself – even if you don't get it right the first time. That's why snowboarding is a fantastic way to learn and develop a new interest. I met Kathy Champion, 15, on Mont Blanc, where she explained why snowboarding is a great benefit for teens.

(1) _____ At only nine years old, she was already snowboarding with her dad in Scotland and she continues to love it to this day. 'Being in the mountains for hours every day made me feel so healthy and alive,' she says. It helped her to understand how her body works because she learned techniques to help her to ride the snowboard properly. **(2)** _____ 'Snowboarding taught me to believe in myself, even when I was worried about hurting myself.' Did she get hurt? 'Yes, once or twice, nothing serious,' she says.

'**(3)** _____ It made me want to succeed even more and get to the bottom of the mountain!'

In what other ways can snowboarding make you healthy and enjoy life more? 'It keeps you very fit, very positive, but it also helps you to make new friends,' Kathy says. **(4)** _____ 'You have support from people who understand what you're doing and are there to help you improve.' And she thinks the feel-good part of snowboarding can also help teenagers keep out of trouble. 'Some people I know from school laugh at me when I tell them how great I feel after snowboarding. **(5)** _____ ' So, what is Kathy's advice? 'Get a snowboard, get healthy – and enjoy life!'

2 Five sentences have been removed from the article. Choose from sentences A–H the one which fills each gap (1–5). There are three extra sentences which you do not need to use.

A But it didn't make me stop.
B Kathy started snowboarding at a young age.
C She believes that doing an extreme sport also introduces you to a new and positive community.
D She knew she was going to be good at snowboarding.
E She already understood how to ride a snowboard.
F It also made her feel that she could do something very well.
G They think that hanging out on the street and doing stupid things is fun – I don't see how!
H She feels teenagers think it is too dangerous to try snowboarding.

3 Match the highlighted words in the text to their meanings.

1 achieve something you want to do
2 something someone tells you to help you
3 ways of doing something well
4 feel pain because of an accident
5 an advantage from doing something

4 Complete the sentences with the highlighted words from the text.

1 You have to work very hard to _____ .
2 I never fall off my bike and _____ .
3 The _____ of doing a new sport is that you learn new skills.
4 I surf every day and have learned the best _____ .
5 My _____ to you is – start snowboarding now!

1 Complete the sentences with *was*, *were*, *wasn't* or *weren't*.

1 The man .... walking to work because it was a lovely day.
2 What .... you doing last night when I tried to call you?
3 I .... studying really hard last night.
4 The boys .... playing tennis – it was volleyball!
5 .... you watching TV at 8 pm last night?
6 What .... your sister doing at lunchtime?
7 I .... playing on your computer yesterday. I was out on my bike.
8 We .... listening to you – can you say it again, please?

2 Write the words in the correct order to make sentences.

1 when / computer / was / games / rang / phone / Chris / the / playing

2 you / visiting / texted / Were / I / grandparents / you? / your / when

3 arms / cat / I / when / from / it / jumped / the / carrying / my / was

4 bedroom / found / I / cleaning / diary / was / my / when / old / my / I

5 hockey / We / rained / going / match / were / the / but / to / it / watch

6 exams / music / while / listening / revising / to / for / They / their / were

7 talking / Were / Peter / maths / the / you / about / to / test?

8 was / you / thinking / called / you / when / I / about / just

3 Choose the correct sentence in each pair.

1 a On her way home, she saw a deer that is standing beside the road eating grass.
  b On her way home, she saw a deer that was standing beside the road eating grass.
2 a I was planing to have a picnic on Saturday.
  b I was planning to have a picnic on Saturday.
3 a He was playing basketball alone.
  b He was play basketball alone.
4 a I first met him at primary school, while we was playing football.
  b I first met him at primary school, while we were playing football.
5 a I was studying at her school until last year, but then I moved.
  b I was studing at her school until last year, but then I moved.

4 Complete the sentences with the correct past form of the verbs in brackets.

1 John .... in the sea when he saw a dolphin. (swim)
2 I .... a film when my sister arrived. (watch)
3 .... to the sports centre when I saw you yesterday? (go)
4 We .... to make you feel bad! (not try)
5 When I went into the classroom, the teacher .... for me. (wait)
6 The DJ .... some great music at the party. (play)
7 Everybody .... during the comedy show. (laugh)
8 Dave .... in New Zealand when he passed his driving test. (live)
9 My brother .... his homework when Mum phoned. (do)
10 Helen .... for a big tennis competition yesterday. (prepare)

1 Complete the sentences with the correct form of the words in the box. Use each word twice.

coach	exercise	fit	match
point	train	trainer	work out

0 The ......*coach*...... talked to the team for an hour, and then we got on the ......*coach*...... and travelled to the stadium.
1 After you've finished your English ...., you should go outside and do some ....
2 I love the colour of these ...., and the athletics club .... said they are the best ones.
3 We have our big .... next week – so we have to buy .... shorts and tops.
4 Simon .... to the clock – the game was finished! And we won by one ....!
5 This sweatshirt .... me well, doesn't it? Now I need to do some exercise to get ....!
6 We have to .... how the other team is going to play. .... more will also help us to win.
7 After .... we can catch the .... home.

2 Complete the sentences with the correct form of the words from Exercise 1.

1 That skirt doesn't _____ – it's too big!
2 Our team won by three _____ – 29–26. Hurray!
3 Next week it's the final football _____ of this year.
4 Our tennis _____ wants us to practise for two hours every day.
5 What size are your _____?
6 These science _____ our teacher gave us for homework are so hard!

LISTENING

1 Read the poster. What does it mean?

1 A new sports centre opened last week.
2 If you go on Saturday, you will have to pay.
3 On Saturday you can try different sports for free.

BANK SPORTS CENTRE

OPENING SOON!

COME ALONG AND HAVE A GO AT SOME NEW SPORTS!

OPEN DAY SATURDAY 9 AM – 4 PM
BRING A FRIEND AND HAVE FUN! FREE ENTRY!

2 Listen to the radio podcast. Tick (✓) the things they talk about.

1 what makes the Bank Sports Centre different ☐
2 more information about new sports ☐
3 if there are team sports ☐
4 sports that use a ball ☐
5 summer activities ☐
6 the open day ☐
7 opening times ☐

3 Listen again. Are these sentences true (T) or false (F)?

1 There's a gym at the sports centre. _____
2 The room for hot yoga is 44 °C. _____
3 There is a type of yoga you can do in the air. _____
4 In the winter, you can do ice skating. _____
5 In the summer, they put sand down for summer sports. _____
6 The open day means only members can go along. _____
7 There will be prizes on Saturday. _____

4 Listen again and complete the information.

1	Name of sports centre	
2	Popular activities	swimming, classes and
3	Two types of yoga	and yoga in the air
4	New winter sports	
5	New summer sport	
6	Open day for	

5 Listen again. How did the people say the following?

1 The Bank Sports Centre is similar to all sports centres.

2 We want people to try out different sports.

3 It's enjoyable.

4 What sport can I do that I haven't done before?

5 Bring everyone – any age!

6 It doesn't cost any money.

VOCABULARY Crimes and criminals

1 Write the letters in the correct order to make crime words.

1 l u g r r a y b ....
2 v a i m s n a l d ....
3 e t f h t ....
4 g i s o h i l t n p f ....
5 c o p i p n g c e t i k k ....
6 a g i h c k n ....

2 Match the words in Exercise 1 to the pictures.

1 ....   4 ....
2 ....   5 ....
3 ....   6 ....

3 Match the definition with the type of crime from Exercise 1.

1 when someone enters another person's house without asking and takes their things ....
2 when someone takes something from another person's bag or pocket without them knowing ....
3 when someone takes something from a shop without paying for it ....
4 when someone enters someone else's computer system and takes information without them knowing ....
5 when someone damages private or public buildings or things ....
6 when someone dishonestly takes another person's things and keeps them ....

4 Choose the correct word to complete the sentence.

1 I really worry about *shoplifters / hackers* reading my emails.
2 I read an article in the paper yesterday about some *vandals / burglars* in the city centre breaking windows.
3 *Pickpockets / Burglars* don't care that when they enter someone's house and take their things, it can have a huge emotional effect.
4 There are signs everywhere on the metro telling passengers to be careful with their bags, as there are lots of *hackers / pickpockets*.
5 They put cameras in the office after *a thief / a shoplifter* stole a lot of money from an employee's desk.
6 Mrs Santana caught the *burglars / shoplifters* who were trying to steal mobile phones from her shop.

5 Complete the sentences with the correct forms of the crimes and criminals.

1 A .... stole millions of dollars from people's bank accounts. Security teams at the banks say .... is a very serious problem in the United States.
2 After breaking the windows and putting paint on the door, the two .... ran away. One .... was wearing a black hat.
3 I'd like to report a .... I arrived home tonight to find a .... in my kitchen with a bag full of my things.
4 I watched the .... as they put their hands inside people's bags and pockets and took their money. .... happens a lot in some big cities.
5 The police say that car .... has increased since 2014. The .... are usually between the ages of 18 and 35.
6 The local shop has a few .... who steal their chocolate bars. The police are often called there because of ....

1 Read the blog quickly. What is the author doing?

  a explaining that all types of hackers send spam emails
  b explaining that all types of hackers want to make money
  c explaining that different types of hackers have different reasons for hacking

Hacking

Hacking has been in the news a lot recently, and is a growing problem all over the world. But did you know that there are different types of hackers out there, with different aims? At first, I thought that these people were all just criminals trying to make money. I thought that they were the people who are responsible for those nasty emails I get in my inbox or for stealing money from people's bank accounts.

But then I did some research on the internet. I found out that there are different types of hackers, and each one has different reasons for hacking. Here is what I found out about some of the different types of hackers:

White Hat Hacker

This type of hacker is a professional hacker who works for companies and governments. These hackers are allowed to use their skills to hack computer systems so that the company or government can repair any weaknesses in its own system before another hacker tries to enter the system for criminal reasons.

Black Hat Hacker

This is the type of hacker that you usually read about in news stories. These hackers enter computer systems illegally to steal companies' or people's money and information. They also attack computer systems so that they stop working, and send spam emails.

Grey Hat Hacker

This type of hacker is between a White Hat Hacker and a Black Hat Hacker. Sometimes, these hackers find weaknesses in a computer system and repair it for the company for free. Other times they find the weaknesses and then tell the company about them and offer to repair them for cash.

Hacktivists

These people are different from the other types of hackers. They don't hack to make money or to find weaknesses in computer systems, but instead they have social or political reasons for hacking. They usually enter the computer systems of big companies and governments to steal their information.

So now you know that not all hackers are the same. Did any of this surprise you? Leave a comment, and tell me what you think!

2 Read the blog again. Decide if each sentence is true (T) or false (F).

  1 At first the author didn't know that there were different types of hackers.
  2 White Hat Hackers are criminals.
  3 Black Hat Hackers help companies and governments to fix their computer systems.
  4 Grey Hat Hackers always ask for money to fix weaknesses in computer systems.
  5 Hacktivists don't have the same reasons for hacking as the other types of hackers.
  6 Companies and governments pay hacktivists to steal information for them.

3 Match the highlighted words in the text to their meanings.

  1 results that you want to achieve ....
  2 money ....
  3 very bad or not nice ....
  4 parts of something that are not strong or good ....
  5 emails that you do not want, especially advertisements ....

GRAMMAR Past simple and continuous

1 Choose the best answer in each sentence.

1 What were you doing when the pickpocket stole your wallet?
   a I listened to music and sent a text message.
   b I was listening to music and sending a text message.

2 Who were you talking to this morning?
   a My mum. She phoned because she wanted me to buy some bread.
   b My mum was phoning me because she wanted me to buy some bread.

3 What happened to your computer?
   a I was playing a game and it was hacked.
   b I played a game and it was hacked.

4 Did you see what the burglar looked like?
   a No, it was dark. He ran away.
   b No, it was dark. He was run away.

5 Did you hear the doorbell?
   a No, I was sleeping.
   b No, I slept.

2 Make sentences using the past simple or past continuous.

1 I / answer questions / about / vandals / at the police station.

2 Those boys / steal / money / from my bag.

3 Mum / tell / us / a story about / Grandma / when / her phone / ring.

4 Mark / not wave / at Julie / because / he / not / see her.

5 In the newspaper / it say / that in our city / theft / increase / this year.

3 Complete the conversation with the past simple or past continuous form of the verbs in the box.

| be | get | imagine | look | love |
| run | see | sing | take | think |

A: That's a good photo. Tell me about it!
B: I ¹_____ late for school and I ²_____ down the road. It was a beautiful day and the birds ³_____. I ⁴_____ about my English homework. I had to write a story about a photo. I didn't know what to write. You know, when you have no ideas! But then I ⁵_____ up and I ⁶_____ this amazing graffiti art on the wall near the supermarket! I ⁷_____ out my phone and ⁸_____ a photo.
A: Did you write about it for your homework?
B: I did! I ⁹_____ the lives of the graffiti artists. Some people think they are criminals; some don't. That's what interested me. My teacher ¹⁰_____ the story! I got a great mark!

4 Correct the mistakes in these sentences or tick (✓) any you think are correct.

1 They steal chocolate from the shop when I saw them.

2 On Saturday, although it was raining, I went to the fun fair with my friends.

3 We were sitting on the bus when the vandals write on the windows.

4 It snowed when I woke up this morning.

5 I arrived home in the morning, but then I was sleeping all day.

VOCABULARY ourselves, yourselves, themselves and each other

1 Match the questions and answers.

1 What happened to Jill's hand? _____
2 Who cut your hair? _____
3 What are those boys doing? _____
4 How was football practice? _____
5 What do Zoe and Carter think of the song they recorded together? _____

a I did it myself! Do you like it?
b They haven't heard it yet! They say they don't like listening to themselves.
c They're arguing with each other.
d She burned herself while she was cooking.
e It was good! We all enjoyed ourselves.

2 Complete the conversations with the correct pronoun.

1 **A:** Where did you two get those jeans?
   B: We made them _____.
2 **A:** Can your dad speak Spanish?
   B: Yes, a bit. He taught _____ last year before our holiday.
3 **A:** What are those girls doing?
   B: They're taking photos of _____ together.
4 **A:** We're thirsty. Can we have a glass of water?
   B: Sure, help _____.
5 **A:** Zane and Christina speak really good French!
   B: Yes, they speak French to _____ all the time!

1 Have you or anyone you know been burgled? What happened?

2 Read Michael's story. Is Michael's story similar to yours or different?

It was midnight, and I was watching a film when I heard a loud knock at the door. 'That's strange,' I thought. 'Who could it be?' I was a bit worried because I was by myself, so I quietly walked downstairs and stood by the front door to listen for any noise outside. I looked through the window but couldn't see anyone, so I slowly opened the door – nobody was there. I still felt nervous, but I went back inside to finish watching the film. Almost immediately, I heard another knock. I thought it was someone playing a joke, so I opened the door and walked out onto the street to see if I could see them. I looked up and down the street and after a minute or two returned to my house. I had just started watching the film again, when I heard a noise coming from upstairs. It sounded like there was someone up there moving around. I was really scared, so I ran straight to my neighbours' house for help. After a while, they answered the door, and I asked them to phone the police quickly. They looked at each other with worried faces. They rang the police and said they would come soon. While we were waiting for the police to arrive, we saw two men wearing black jeans and coats come out of my house with big bags full of things. They got into a car and drove away quickly. Not long after, the police arrived and checked my house. My mum's jewellery, my computer and some cash I had in my room were missing. The police never caught the burglars, and we never got our stuff back. It was a nasty experience, but I tell myself that I had a lucky escape.

3 Tick (✓) the topics that Michael included.

1 what time the burglary took place ☐
2 how many burglars there were ☐
3 what they were wearing ☐
4 how the burglars got away ☐
5 who called the police ☐
6 what damage the burglars caused ☐
7 what the burglars took ☐
8 how much money they stole ☐

4 Look at the highlighted words in Michael's story. Which are adjectives and which are adverbs? Add two more of your own to each group.

Adjectives	Adverbs

5 Complete the sentences with an adjective or adverb from Exercise 4.

1 I was so scared. I called the police
....

2 The neighbours said the music was too
....

3 I said goodbye to Ella and that I would see her
....

4 It was hard to hear him – he talked very
....

5 The horror film last night made me feel
....

6 The book is complicated, so you have to read it
....

6 Prepare to write a story.

Read the task. Then plan your ideas, and make some notes.

> Your English teacher has asked you to write a story.
> Your story must begin with this sentence:
> *I knocked on the door and waited.*

7 Write your story.

✓
- Write about 100 words.
- Make sure there is a beginning, middle and end.
- Give the story an interesting title.
- Use verbs in the past simple and past continuous.
- Use adjectives and adverbs to make your story interesting
- Remember to check your spelling and grammar.

6 CITY LIFE

1 Complete the crossword using the clues below.

1 dirty air in towns and cities
2 buses and trains that people pay to travel on
3 a long line of vehicles waiting to move
4 large numbers of people in one place
5 words or pictures that we see on walls
6 the busiest period in a city for traffic
7 areas of grass and trees in a city
8 things some people don't want and leave on the street
9 when an electrical system stops working

2 Choose the correct words to complete the sentences.

1 The city is full of *pollution / rubbish*, so the government is asking people to stop driving their cars for one day.
2 I was in a *power cut / traffic jam*, so I got home late.
3 People leave their *rubbish / crowds* on the street and it makes the city look horrible.
4 There are lots of *green spaces / public transport* in my city where you can relax and have lunch.
5 The *graffiti / crowds* at the concert last night were really big.
6 *Public transport / Rush hour* in my town is very good. I always get to work on time.
7 Some people think *graffiti / green spaces* is not really art.
8 We had no electricity for six hours because there was a *rush hour / power cut*.
9 I leave work early every day, so I miss the *rush hour / public transport*.

3 Complete the conversations with the words from Exercise 1.

Anna: Have you seen that new
¹ _____ on
the wall of Central Tower? It's an
amazing work of art!

Nathan: Yeah, I don't like it. I think it
makes the city look untidy. And
if that isn't bad enough, people
still don't use bins and leave their
² _____ on the
streets.

Anna: Oh, I love it! But I know what
you mean about the city
looking untidy. We need more
³ _____ to
make it look more beautiful and
natural.

Nathan: Yeah, but what can we do about
the ⁴ _____?
The air is really dirty!

Anna: I know! There are too many cars
on the road – I'm always in a
⁵ _____ trying
to get home.

Nathan: Don't remind me! When
I leave work at 5 pm, it's
⁶ _____, and
driving then is the worst!

Anna: I agree, but it's the
same when you use
⁷ _____ – there
are ⁸ _____
of people everywhere waiting for
buses and trains. You can't move!

Nathan: It was like that last week. There
was a ⁹ _____
for a few hours – no street lights,
no trains or buses. People didn't
get home until 10 pm!

READING

1 Read about these green cities. Write the topics mentioned in the correct column of the table. Sometimes more than one column is correct.

| animal life | bicycles | parks | pollution | public transport | recycling | rubbish |

Barcelona	Bogotá	Singapore	Adelaide

Talking about green cities around the world

More than half the world's population now lives in cities. The populations of cities are getting bigger and pollution is getting worse. So which cities are trying to solve this? We asked you which cities you think are the greenest.

I chose Barcelona because I **(1)** _____ it's a great example of a green city. There are lots of buses here and people often ride their bike to school or walk. There is also a metro system and cable cars. I think that the pollution from cars is a really big **(2)** _____, so Barcelona is a green city because it encourages people to take other forms of **(3)** _____ instead of their cars. Also, there are lots of parks in the **(4)** _____ of the city because it strongly believes in keeping the city green and healthy. The parks have lots of grass and trees and the air **(5)** _____ is very good. People **(6)** _____ to them to relax, to have lunch or to play sport.
Calen

Singapore is a green city in Asia. I think something like 30% of the city is covered by trees and green spaces. The trees help to reduce the hot temperatures and noise from traffic, giving people who live in Singapore a better quality of life. Even the airport is green because there are gardens and a butterfly farm. That's so smart! In the past, there was a lot of pollution but now Singapore wants to be famous for being green. I found a website about green things in Singapore and things you can do. You can pick up the rubbish in your area with your friends. I think it's great and people learn that it's not good to leave rubbish on the street.
Winston

Bogotá in Colombia is an interesting city because in 2016 it had a week where no cars were allowed into the city. There were buses but not many taxis. The city has also had 'Cycle Sunday' for over 30 years. The roads become bicycle paths. I think that's really cool because then you really think about the environment. The idea is that there is less pollution and everyone has to get into town in a 'green' way – walking, cycling, or bus. The idea was so successful that the mayor decided to create 300 km of bicycle lanes, which increased bicycle use by five times in the city. There's a good reason for it being called 'the greenest city in Latin America'!
Poppy

I didn't think Australia had a lot of pollution, but it does. Adelaide in South Australia is a green city. There are 29 parks and there's a big hotel there which recycles its energy and water. Also, there are a lot of cycle paths and you can hire a bike for free. That's really good. There is a bus that doesn't use petrol: it is solar powered – you know, it uses energy from the sun! That's awesome!
Kelly

2 Read the paragraph about Barcelona again.
For each question, choose the correct answer.

1	**A** imagine	**B** guess	**C** think	**D** wonder
2	**A** complication	**B** problem	**C** operation	**D** situation
3	**A** transport	**B** vehicle	**C** travel	**D** movement
4	**A** middle	**B** inside	**C** zone	**D** area
5	**A** standard	**B** condition	**C** quality	**D** level
6	**A** visit	**B** arrive	**C** go	**D** move

3 Which writer

1 was surprised by some information? _____
2 likes that one kind of transport does not cost any money? _____
3 thinks an idea is intelligent? _____
4 likes an idea because it makes people think about the environment? _____
5 thinks people need to learn to be tidy? _____
6 thinks it's a good idea to reuse things? _____

some/any, much/many, a lot of,
a few / a little

1 Complete the sentences with *some* or *any*.

1 She received .... beautiful flowers in hospital.
2 I haven't got .... money.
3 You don't have to pay for .... of the buses – they're all free!
4 There are .... places I really don't want to visit.

2 Complete the sentences with *much* or *many*.

1 I haven't got .... time – what do you want?
2 Felix didn't buy .... biscuits.
3 Did that phone cost .... ?
4 It's my first day – I don't know .... people.

3 Complete the sentences with *a little* or *a few*.

1 Help yourself to .... pieces of paper.
2 There's .... cake left – would you like it?
3 I just want .... information about the town, please.
4 Wait here – there are .... things I need to get from the shop.

4 Choose the correct option.

1 Our capital city has .... pollution.
 a a lot of **b** many **c** a few
2 There are .... really beautiful green spaces in Vancouver.
 a any **b** much **c** some
3 Jessie never has .... money. It's really annoying.
 a many **b** a little **c** any
4 There are .... interesting things to do in this town.
 a any **b** many **c** much
5 There are .... people here who don't put their rubbish in the bin.
 a a few **b** little **c** any
6 There isn't .... we can do now – just wait for the power cut to end!
 a many **b** a little **c** much
7 I can speak .... German.
 a a few **b** a little **c** much
8 Pablo moved to my school last week and he doesn't have .... friends yet.
 a many **b** much **c** some
9 Would you like .... coffee?
 a a few **b** some **c** much
10 I'm nearly out of the traffic jam – I'll be home in .... minutes.
 a a little **b** any **c** a few

5 Read the text and choose the correct word.

The Whitsunday Islands are a group of islands in the middle of the Great Barrier Reef. [1]*Many / Much* of them don't have [2]*any / some* facilities, so you can't stay there, but there are [3]*some / a little* that have [4]*a few / a little* hotels. [5]*Much / A lot of* Australians like to spend their holidays on these islands because they are beautiful. If you need to relax, they are perfect because there isn't [6]*much / many* to do except swim in the beautiful blue sea. So all you need is [7]*a few / a little* time to book your next holiday in paradise!

6 Look at the picture and choose the correct options to complete the text.

It's Cycle Day in Newtown and there are [1]*any / many / much* bicycles for hire. Today's the day to go for a bike ride, so there aren't [2]*any / many / some* people walking, and although we can see [3]*a few / a little / much* tables at the café, they are empty. We can see [4]*a little / a lot of / much* flags in the picture. There's a wall with [5]*any / many / some* graffiti on it but not [6]*many / much / some*. There aren't [7]*any / a few / a lot of* animals in the picture.

7 Choose the correct sentence in each pair.

1 **a** On my first day at a new school, I didn't have friends.
 b On my first day at a new school, I didn't have any friends.
2 **a** I went to the beach and I had a lot of fun.
 b I went to the beach and I had much fun.
3 **a** We can have lunch in a tent near the lake.
 b We can have lunch in some tent near the lake.
4 **a** Few hours later, they had to go back.
 b A few hours later, they had to go back.
5 **a** We do a lot of things together.
 b We do alot of things together.

VOCABULARY — Compounds: noun + noun

1 Add the missing vowels (a, e, i, o, u) to complete these words.

1 __ p __ r t m __ n t
   b __ __ l d __ n g
2 p __ s t b __ x
3 s p __ __ __ d l __ m __ t
4 t __ x __ r __ n k
5 p __ d __ s t r __ __ __ n
   c r __ s s __ n g
6 r __ c y c l __ n g b __ n
7 b __ s s t __ p
8 r __ __ d s __ g n

2 Complete the sentences with the singular or plural form of a compound noun from Exercise 1. Use each compound noun once.

1 You need to look left and right at the
   .... before
   you walk.
2 The .... tells you
   how to get to the town centre.
3 .... for glass in my
   country are yellow.
4 Look! The ....
   here is 20 km per hour. Slow down!
5 We live on the ground floor of the
   ....
6 The number 65 stops at the
   .... opposite
   the cinema.
7 They empty our
   .... every day to
   take the letters.
8 You wait at the ....
   and then tell the driver where you want
   to go.

LISTENING

1 Tick (✓) the things you can clean up.

1 bedroom ☐   5 computer ☐
2 river ☐   6 house ☐
3 burgers ☐   7 bag ☐
4 desk ☐   8 writing ☐

◀)) 03 2 Listen to a teacher introducing a class project. What are the students going to talk about?

1 how to clean their classroom
2 something they want to clean
3 interesting clean-up projects

◀)) 04 3 Now listen to the full conversation and complete the sentences with one word in each space.

1 Jenny talks about a project that is a ....
   for children on an Australian website.
2 Jenny chose a .... for a form of transport.
3 Jenny liked it because it teaches children about a
   .... in a fun way.
4 Greg's project is about cleaning up a ....
   in the USA.
5 Greg found it on the .... of an American
   history museum.

◀)) 05 4 Listen to another student, Meg, talking about her project. Complete the text with one word in each space.

Well, I actually took part in a 'clean-up [1] ....
beach' day. There was a big [2] .... of people
and we all [3] .... at the bus stop in front of the
beach. There was a man who [4] .... us what to
do. We had big [5] .... bags and we collected
any [6] .... that we found. We were in different
[7] .... and we worked together.
It was a really [8] .... day but it's a pity people
[9] .... all this rubbish. It's easy to put it in the
[10] .... !

◀)) 06 5 Listen to the conversations again. Are these sentences true (T) or false (F)?

1 Jenny talked about a game for adults. ....
2 You have to do something for the
   environment in the game. ....
3 Jenny learned things by playing the game. ....
4 She thinks she and her friends should
   do something similar. ....
5 Greg visited the museum to help clean
   it up. ....
6 The teacher liked both Jenny's and
   Greg's projects. ....
7 Meg's project was about cleaning up
   bus stops. ....

7 GETTING ON

VOCABULARY *be, do, have* and *make*

1 Choose the correct verb in each sentence.

1 It _____ me angry when my sister goes into my bedroom.
   a makes   **b** does   **c** has
2 Vicki is _____ problems with her maths homework – can you help?
   a making   **b** doing   **c** having
3 My brother and I _____ an argument this evening about washing the dishes.
   a made   **b** had   **c** did
4 When you called yesterday, I _____ on my own.
   a was   **b** had   **c** have
5 Do you want to _____ something for Dad's birthday?
   a be   **b** do   **c** have
6 We always _____ fun at Annie's house – she has a swimming pool!
   a have   **b** make   **c** are
7 Can you _____ me a favour?
   a do   **b** make   **c** have
8 I _____ lots of new friends at my new school.
   a did   **b** made   **c** was
9 My dad _____ annoyed with me for not doing my homework.
   a had   **b** did   **c** was
10 I really like Mary – we _____ lots in common.
   a do   **b** have   **c** make

2 Match the questions and answers and add the correct form of the verb.

be	be	do	have	have	make

1 What's the matter with John?
2 Did you break this?
3 Do you get on with your cousin?
4 Is that Phil and his dad over there?
5 Do you want to go for a run?
6 Are you OK?

a Not really, but we can _____ something when you get back.
b Not really. We don't _____ anything in common.
c Well sort of, but it _____ my fault.
d Yes, but this TV show _____ me really angry.
e I think he just wants to _____ on his own for a while.
f Yes! They're _____ an argument about the football!

3 Choose the correct phrase.

1 I'm going to *have fun / have problems with* at the party tonight!
2 Can you *do me a favour / do something* and wake me up at 7 am?
3 I can sometimes *be wrong / be my fault* – I know that!
4 She never listens to her parents – it's not surprising they *are annoyed with / make friends* her.
5 I'm *having problems with / being wrong* my computer.
6 I sometimes enjoy *being on my own / making me angry*.

4 Complete the text with the words and phrases in the box.

angry	argument	fault
friends	in common	on my own
something	wrong	

This morning I woke up late. It wasn't my
¹ _____ – the alarm clock didn't go off. I got up quickly and wanted to go into the bathroom, but my sister was there. She takes a long time every morning and it makes me ² _____. I knocked on the door, but there was no answer. Then we had an ³ _____ because she said she only has a three-minute shower. I don't think so! But she finally came out. I quickly had a shower and breakfast, and then caught the bus – just in time. I'm usually ⁴ _____ on the bus because it's hard to make ⁵ _____ – I don't think I have anything ⁶ _____ with the people at my school. But at the next bus stop, a boy my age got on the bus and he looked like me – unhappy. I asked him if something was ⁷ _____.
'My sister!' he replied. We started chatting and soon we planned to do ⁸ _____ together after school. I'm glad I woke up late!

READING

1 Read the first paragraph quickly. Tick (✓) what you think the article is going to be about.

1 interesting activities you do with your grandparents ☐
2 how you feel about your grandparents ☐
3 arguments with your grandparents ☐

2 Read the whole text and check your answers to Exercise 1.

3 Read the text again. Are these sentences true (T) or false (F)?

1 All of the readers get on very well with their grandparents. ......
2 Giuliana's grandmother lives in a different town. ......
3 Giuliana shares an interest with her grandmother. ......
4 Giuliana's grandmother is teaching her to cook a dish she invented. ......
5 Andy's granddad is good at sports. ......
6 Andy's and Boris's granddads make them laugh. ......
7 Boris's grandfather is a serious man. ......
8 Boris's grandparents don't visit as often as they did. ......

4 Match the highlighted words in the text to their meanings.

1 childish or not serious ......
2 doing things with your face that make people laugh ......
3 in or to a foreign country ......
4 having a thing, experience or emotion at the same time as someone else ......
5 notices or understands something ......
6 food prepared as part of a meal ......

5 Complete the sentences with the correct form of the words from Exercise 4.

1 This .... smells delicious! Yum!
2 Stop being .... ! It's not funny.
3 I love .... music and videos on Facebook with my friends.
4 She's so funny when she ....
5 Alex and his family always go .... in the summer.
6 They didn't .... the train was at noon.

Last month we asked you to send us your ideas about grandparents. We received some very interesting answers! Some of you describe your grandparents as friends. They are the people you talk to when you have to talk to an adult, but you don't want to talk to your mum or dad. They help you, they're there for you and they don't disagree with you. But there are a few of you who have grandparents who live in different towns, or even abroad, and so you don't see them very often.

Grandparents are special people and we love ours! Here's what you say.

Giuliana Ross, Canada
I love everyone in my family, but my grandma is really special for me. She lives a few streets away from us, so when I want to be on my own, I usually walk to her house. She doesn't ask questions. I love that! We do lots of things together too, like making food, which we enjoy. At the moment, she's teaching me to make her favourite dish, which her grandmother taught her. It's quite hard to do, but I love sharing moments with her. It's special.

Andy Davidson, USA
I love my granddad! He's just the best – he can keep a secret, he helps me and he's really funny! We have lots of fun, and we have lots in common. We both enjoy going climbing! My granddad is really good at that – no one realises that he's in his sixties!

Boris Sanneh, UK
My grandparents live in another country. They visit us about every three years, but it's hard because we don't really know what to talk about. They ask about school and things like that. That's usually the first week. By the second week though, things are a bit better and it's more 'natural'. When my sister and I were younger, they visited more often and I remember Grandpa doing silly things, like making faces when Mum wasn't looking. He still does that sometimes. But now that they are older, I'd like them to live closer.

Next week:
Older brothers and sisters – do you get on well? Write in with your experiences to portia@yourteenmag.uk.

GRAMMAR *have to, must* and *should*

1 Write the words in the correct order to make sentences.

1 has / practise / piano / to / the / Zoe / every day

....

2 library / be / You / must / in / quiet / the

....

3 mustn't / in / room / run / dining / the / You

....

4 had / to / Grandma / 5 km / cycle / school / to

....

5 don't / We / to / have / tomorrow / school / to / go

....

6 lunch / to / my / I / make / had / own / yesterday

....

2 Choose the best answer in each sentence.

1 Johnny left basketball class early last week – he .... do his homework.
   a had to   **b** must   **c** didn't have to

2 When you see your brother, you .... tell him about his secret birthday party!
   a don't have to   **b** must   **c** mustn't

3 When the film starts, you .... be quiet.
   a don't have to   **b** had to   **c** must

4 Mum .... wear glasses to read – she can't see properly without them.
   a must   **b** has to   **c** didn't have to

5 I think you .... tell us what happened.
   a should   **b** didn't have to   **c** mustn't

6 Mike and Tracey .... get up early tomorrow – it's the holidays!
   a don't have to   **b** doesn't have to   **c** mustn't

7 Thank you! That's a lovely present, but you .... get me anything!
   a don't have to   **b** didn't have to   **c** mustn't

8 You .... argue so much! It isn't good.
   a must   **b** have to   **c** shouldn't

9 You .... be late for school or make the teacher angry.
   a don't have to   **b** mustn't   **c** should

10 I wasn't sure what to write for my school project, so I asked Dad what I .... do.
   a should   **b** have to   **c** must

3 Complete the sentences with *should* or *shouldn't*.

1 You .... go to bed early when you have school the next day.

2 You .... eat a lot of fast food – it's bad for you.

3 You .... find someone to ask about your homework.

4 The teacher is annoyed with Erik – he .... behave better in class.

5 I .... really play these computer games – they are a waste of time!

6 We .... make a reservation at the restaurant for your birthday dinner.

4 Correct the mistakes in these sentences or tick (✓) any you think are correct.

1 You will bring a ball if you want to play football.

....

2 I have to prepare for the picnic.

....

3 It must be fun if we go together.

....

4 The rules of this game are that you should help the monkey to find her home.

....

5 So you must to believe me – this game is the best.

....

VOCABULARY Phrasal verbs: relationships

1 Write the letters in the correct order to make phrasal verbs.

1 ghan tuo   ....

2 etg no   ....

3 teg tethoerg   ....

4 lafl tou   ....

5 pltis pu   ....

6 kolo refta   ....

7 amek pu   ....

8 moce onarud   ....

2 Complete the text message using the correct form of the verbs in Exercise 1.

Hi James! I'm glad you are
¹.......................... well with your new friend, Philippe. He's a nice person and I think it's great that you're helping him, especially as he
².......................... with his girlfriend the other day. Have you heard about Gina and François? They ³..........................
about something, but I think they'll
⁴.......................... and be friends again soon. ⁵..........................
to my house on Saturday if you like and we'll work on the project. I'm
⁶.......................... my baby sister until 2 pm. But after that, we can meet with Tom for a game of snooker and then
⁷.......................... with everyone else in town. I think we should invite François and Gina too! They're really nice to
⁸.......................... with. What do you think? Text me back today!

1 Read the email from Jamal. When is Max going to visit him? How many questions does he ask Zoe?

To: Zoe Anderson   Reply Forward
From: Jamal Shahin

Hi Zoe,

Great! — My cousin Max is coming to stay with me this summer. I'm so excited!

I don't know what the weather will be like, so it's difficult to tell him what we're going to do! What type of activities do you think we should do together? — Suggest some indoor and outdoor activities

Should I take him to meet my friends? — Yes, he'd like that!

Yes, suggest ... — Should we go to a museum in town?

I'm really happy he's coming to stay!

Write soon,
Jamal

2 Read Zoe's reply to Jamal. Does she answer all of Jamal's questions?

To: Jamal Shahin   Reply Forward
From: Zoe Anderson

Hi Jamal,

It's great to hear from you. I'm glad that your cousin is coming to stay with you this summer.

Everybody loves playing video games, so I think that's a good idea. Also, who doesn't love films? Find a few good movies and watch them together.

You should get together with some of our mates at the park for a game of football. You should also take your cousin to the outdoor swimming pool if it's sunny one day.

I think it's a good idea to go to a museum together. You could go to the Local History Museum on Hamilton Street and learn about the history of our town.

I'm really looking forward to meeting him!

Bye for now,
Zoe

3 Read Zoe's email again and put the ideas in order. Write the numbers 1–5.

a advice for outdoor activities ....
b excited to receive the message ....
c advice for indoor activities ....
d advice for a museum to visit ....
e saying she's excited to meet Max ....

4 Complete the sentences with the correct word.

1 It's .... to hear from you.
2 When the weather is bad, it's a good .... to play video games.
3 You .... go to the cinema to see a film.
4 I'm really looking .... to hanging out with you.

5 Read the email from Juliette.

To: Reply Forward
From: Juliette

Hi,

Next week I'll be with you in London! I can't wait. It's going to be so cool! We can do lots of exciting things together. I need to pack for my trip. What should I bring with me? — Things for playing sport

I know some French things are difficult to find in the UK. So do you want me to bring anything from France? — Suggest ...

I'd like to get you a souvenir from where I live. What would you like me to get you? — Tell Juliette what type of souvenir

I'm so excited about the trip! — Me too. I can't wait!

See you soon,
Juliette

6 Prepare to write an email. Read the task and tips. Then plan your ideas and make some notes. Compare your ideas with a partner.

Write your email to Juliette.
* Use all the notes on Juliette's email.
* Remember to answer all of the questions in the email.
* Write about 100 words.
* Remember to check your spelling and grammar.

8 GOING AWAY

VOCABULARY International travel

1 Match the words in the box to their meanings.

| baggage | check-in desk | customs | passport | queue | sign | ticket |

1 the place at an airport where you go to say you have arrived for your flight
2 a document, like a small book, that you need to enter or leave a country
3 a piece of paper that shows you have paid to do something
4 the place where your bags are examined when you are going into a country
5 a notice in a public place which gives information or instructions
6 something that contains your clothes and personal things when you travel
7 a line of people waiting their turn for something

2 Match the words from 1–5 with a–e to make compound nouns.

1 departure ....   **a** check
2 passport ....   **b** hall
3 security ....   **c** gate
4 boarding ....   **d** control
5 baggage ....   **e** pass

3 Choose the correct answer in each sentence.

1 You usually show your .... pass as you get onto the plane.
  a gate   **b** boarding **c** departure
2 Your bags are sometimes opened at the .... check.
  a passport   **b** check-in   **c** security
3 If you don't know where to go in an airport, look at a ....
  a ticket   **b** passport **c** sign
4 You collect your bags from the .... hall when you arrive at your destination.
  a departure **b** baggage **c** security
5 If you are going to a different country, you need a ....
  a sign   **b** passport **c** security check
6 When you are waiting to get on the plane, you stand in a ....
  a sign   **b** customs **c** queue
7 The last place before you get on the plane is the .... gate.
  a departure **b** check-in **c** customs

4 Complete the text with words from Exercises 1 and 2.

So, I'm ready to go and I know what to do! I printed my [1] .... last night and today I added a few things to my [2] .... It weighs exactly 23 kg – I hope it'll be OK when I get to the [3] .... Tomorrow we're getting up at 6 am – Dad's going to drive me to the airport. I have to follow the [4] .... to check-in for Paris. Then I'll go through [5] .... and show my [6] .... and continue through the [7] .... I really hope I don't have to wait in a [8] .... for long because I want to get to the [9] .... quickly. Then I fly to Paris! When I get to Paris, I'll go through [10] .... , then get my bag from the [11] .... and meet up with my cousin, Stefano. He's got the [12] .... for the train to Marseilles! I'm excited … and scared!

1 Read the article quickly. Tick (✓) the best title.

1 How to close your suitcase ☐
2 Going on holiday? What to take and how to take it ☐
3 What not to pack for a holiday ☐

2 Read the article again. Choose the correct answer.

1 The person who wrote the article is
   a a professional writer.
   b a reader.
2 The author says strong bags are a good idea because
   a they travel better.
   b they are often larger.
3 When thinking about the clothes to take, generally she suggests taking
   a more than you think you need.
   b less than you think you need.
4 The article tells you that when you pack for a summer holiday,
   a you need two swimsuits.
   b make sure you have enough shoes.
5 Having lots of bags means
   a you can easily find what you're looking for.
   b you can pack more quickly.
6 You should take things like music and books with you
   a so you don't get bored.
   b to help you relax.
7 The author says it's a good idea to
   a think about what to take just before you go.
   b check that everything will go into your bag.

3 Complete the sentences with the correct form of the highlighted words from the text.

1 If you _____ the pizza _____ the oven now, it'll be ready in 15 minutes.
2 Lush Cola is _____ the sailing race around the world.
3 I bought a pair of shoes, a dress and two _____ in the sales.
4 I've made a _____ so I can listen to music on the beach.
5 Could you pass me the salt please – I can't _____ it from here.

You wrote it!

In this month's article, Portia Plymouth tells us what's she's taking on her summer holiday and how to pack! Great advice, Portia. You have won a £100 voucher to spend at funkybagsforyou.com – a great website that is sponsoring this month's *You wrote it!*

So, you're going on a summer holiday and your mum says you have to pack your bag yourself! What now? Here are some tips for packing that I've learned the hard way!

> First, find out how much you can take – if you are going on a long flight, you can sometimes take more but not always, so it's important to check. Make sure your bag is a strong one of good quality. Once, when I went to get my bag, I realised that it was open! Everyone could see what was in my bag! Oops!

> Find out what you're going to do and what the weather will be like at your destination. Then make a list of all the clothes you plan to take. And then divide that in half, so if you have four tops, take two. One year, I went on holiday and I didn't wear half the clothes I had with me! So ask yourself a few questions, like do you really need five pairs of shoes? (No!) Also, if it's a summer holiday, you're probably going to be wearing your swimsuit most of the time. Make sure you pack two – there's nothing worse than trying to get into a wet swimsuit!

> Do you hate that feeling when you can't find what you're looking for in your bag? Me too! Placing smaller bags inside the bigger bag is the best solution. That way, you can easily reach everything. Also, if you're travelling by plane, don't forget that any liquids have to be in a clear plastic bag.

> You don't want to get bored, so it's essential to take things to keep yourself busy while you're travelling and relaxing by the pool. Don't leave it too late to think about your holiday reading and listening. Create some holiday playlists for your phone and find some new books by your favourite authors. You could also keep a diary so that in the cold winter months you can read about your wonderful summer!

> Don't leave packing until the last moment. Make a list of everything you need about two weeks before. Then get everything ready. You can also pop it in your bag a couple of days before – just check it all fits!

Future: *be going to* and present continuous

1 Write the words in the correct order to make sentences.

1 going / to / next year / visit / Paris / We're

2 clean / to / it's / her / car / going / because / dirty / Mum's

3 are / My / without /holiday / parents / a / Bali / having / in / me / !

4 homework / to / I'm / do / going / my / now

5 is / Tom / buy / going / a / to / phone / new

6 basketball / are / playing / for / the / week / team / James and Noah / school / next

7 going to / our tickets / Zac / for / is / the music festival / to buy / the ticket office

8 sit down / going / of / have / coffee / I'm / a / to / and / cup

2 Complete the conversation with the present continuous or *be going to* form of the verbs in the box.

do	fill in	go	have	return	take

Lily: Hey, Tyler. What ¹_____ later?

Tyler: I ²_____ that form for the summer camp.

Lily: Oh, really? ³_____ camping this year? I didn't think you wanted to go.

Tyler: Yeah, I know, but it was fun last year. And I think they ⁴_____ different sports, like rock climbing. Also, everyone from last year's camp ⁵_____. I can't wait to see Stacie and Jonas!

Lily: Well, I think it sounds great – but I can't go. Mum and Dad ⁶_____ me to an adventure park in the USA this summer.

Tyler: Lucky you!

3 Read the sentences and choose the correct verb.

1 Emilia is *going to visit* / *visiting* her aunt in Australia one day. She needs to save up first!

2 On Monday, the Maz family are *flying* / *going to fly* to the Caribbean for their summer holiday.

3 I think I'm *going to watch* / *watching* TV tonight. I don't want to go out.

4 We're *leaving* / *going to leave* at 5 am tomorrow – don't be late!

5 We're *going to buy* / *buying* new bikes soon.

6 My dad is *going to cook* / *cooking* us a pizza when you next come over.

7 We're *studying* / *going to study* fish in biology next week.

8 Marcia is *going to be* / *being* late to school again.

4 Choose the correct sentence in each pair.

⊚ 1 a Tomorrow we are going to the beach.
   b Tomorrow we go to the beach.

2 a I'm going to visit Paris next year.
   b I'm going visit Paris next year.

3 a We are excited because next Saturday we have a party!
   b We are excited because next Saturday we are having a party!

4 a Next weekend we are going to have a picnic.
   b Next weekend we have a picnic.

5 a Next Saturday my family and I are going to a picnic.
   b Next Saturday my family and I going to a picnic.

5 Complete the sentences with the correct form of the present continuous or *be going to*. Sometimes both are possible.

We've got a long journey ahead to get to Canada. We're **(1)**_____ (catch) the plane at 9.30 tomorrow morning, so I'm **(2)**_____ (find) my old alarm clock tonight! I know we **(3)**_____ (have) a great time! The only problem is that our friends say the weather's not good, so it's probably **(4)**_____ (rain) for some of the time we're there. We're **(5)**_____ (stay) with friends in Montreal for a week and then we're **(6)**_____ (travel) to Toronto on the 15th. It's all planned – and I really can't wait!

1 Make phrasal verbs with a word from box A and a word from box B to match the definitions.

A check   get   go   look
pick   set   take

B around   away   back
in   off   up

1 leave your home to spend time in a different place _____
2 start a journey _____
3 arrive at its destination (transport) _____
4 show your ticket at an airport _____
5 return to a place after you have been somewhere else _____
6 walk in a place you haven't visited before and see new things _____
7 collect someone and take them somewhere in a car _____
8 move from the ground to the air _____

2 Complete the conversation with the correct form of the phrasal verbs from Exercise 1. Add any other words you need.

A: So when [1] _____ ?
B: On Saturday. We [2] _____ at 5 am, I think.
A: Really? Why are you leaving so early?
B: Well, because we are [3] _____ John on the way to the airport in London.
A: Sure, it's still really early though!
B: I know, but we have [4] _____ at the airport at 8 am.
A: What time does the plane [5] _____ for Madrid?
B: 9.30 am and it [6] _____ at 10.30 am.
A: So you have lots of time to see Madrid!
B: Yes! Because we arrive early we can [7] _____ before lunch. So many things to see!
A: Ah, OK. And when are you [8] _____ ?
B: Sunday night sometime.

07 1 You will hear a woman called Elisa Williams telling a group of students about her work as a travel writer. Tick (✓) the topics she mentions.

1 when she became a travel writer ☐
2 where her travel writing appears ☐
3 how much money she makes for her work ☐
4 what she does when she visits places ☐
5 how long it takes her to write an article ☐
6 the best holiday she has ever had ☐
7 places she wants to visit in the future ☐
8 the most difficult part of her job ☐

07 2 For each question, write the correct answer in the gap. Write one or two words, a number, a date or a time.

A travel writer

Elisa has been a full-time travel writer for
(1) _____ years.

Most of Elisa's travel writing appears in
(2) _____ .

Elisa avoids travelling by
(3) _____ if possible.

Elisa always tries to learn a
(4) _____ in every place she visits.

Elisa aims to visit some
(5) _____ in the future.

Elisa says she finds it difficult to write the
(6) _____ of a travel article.

VOCABULARY — Money and shopping

1 Complete the crossword using the clues below.

1 you get this back if you pay more for something than it costs
2 keep money so that you can buy something with it in the future
3 to return something to the place you bought it from
4 a price which is lower than usual
5 give something to someone without asking for payment
6 the place in a shop where you pay for your goods
7 you keep your money in this and take it out when you need to
8 the amount of money that you pay to buy something
9 a piece of paper that proves you have received goods or money

2 Choose the correct words to complete the sentences.

1 My friend is *saving up / taking back* to buy a new phone.
2 I opened a *checkout / bank account* last week to put my money in.
3 Let's go to that new clothes shop – there are lots of *special offers / receipts*.
4 The *change / price* of clothes online is often cheaper than in a shop.
5 This doesn't fit – I'll *take it back / save it up* tomorrow.
6 Helene has got a part-time job at the *checkout / bank account* in our local supermarket.
7 I always *take back / give away* my old clothes to second-hand shops.
8 I gave you £5, so I need £2 *change / checkout* please.
9 I can't return this broken CD – I've lost the *price / receipt*.

3 Complete the conversation with the correct form of the words from Exercise 1.

Daniella: Look at this beautiful new pair of trainers. Oh, and this shop has them on ¹ _____ .

Will: Yeah, that's a really good ² _____ for those trainers. Let's go!

In the shop

Daniella: There they are! OK, cool – with my birthday money I'm sure I have enough ³ _____ , but I'll just check my ⁴ _____ with the app on my phone. Yep! Cool!

Will: OK. Well, time to pay, so let's go to the ⁵ _____ !

(gives money)

Shop assistant: Thank you. Oh wait! That's too much. Here's your ⁶ _____ and your ⁷ _____ . Have a nice day!

Will: Thank you! Don't lose that, Daniella. If you have to ⁸ _____ them _____ , you must have it.

Daniella: Not necessary! They're perfect! Look!

Will: Hope so! If not, you will have to ⁹ _____ them _____ !

READING

1 Read the first paragraph quickly. Tick (✓) what you think the article is going to be about.

1 The best places to shop online. ☐
2 Staying safe when shopping online. ☐
3 Bad stories about people losing money online. ☐

Shopping online

Lots of people enjoy the benefits of online shopping. You don't have to sit in traffic jams or wait at bus stops or at train stations. Because online stores are open 24 hours, seven days a week, you can sit at your computer and shop at your leisure. And you don't have to collect your product because they deliver it right to your door.

But shopping online isn't all great – you need to be very careful when deciding what to buy and where to buy it. Here are some tips for shopping safely online.

 Use a secure connection
The easiest way of making sure the connection is secure is to look for the lock sign in the address bar. Another is to look at the start of the website address. If this starts with 'https', there is a secure connection because the letter 's' means 'secure'. If you see 'http' with no 's', don't enter the website or give your personal or bank details. It could be a false website that is trying to steal your money or personal information.

 Use a secure payment method
Only shop on sites that offer secure payment methods, like credit cards and other payment systems. This gives you protection in a situation where you and the shop disagree – the shop can't say you did anything illegal, like using another person's credit card to pay. Banks usually contact you if they think something is wrong.

 Create a strong password
A strong password is very important. It's usually a good idea to change your passwords every few months, just in case someone finds out what they are. Also, try to use a different password for different online shopping sites: once someone guesses one password, they can get access to everything you do online.

 Check other customers' comments
Always check the seller's history when using online sites. You can get an idea by looking at other buyers' comments. If you are not sure about a product, you can always send the seller a question and the good sellers will reply fairly quickly.

2 Read the article. Choose the correct answers.

1 What is the purpose of the article?
   A to help people save money when shopping online
   B to stop people shopping online
   C to make people think twice before shopping online
   D to help people stay safe when shopping online
2 According to the author, what are the benefits of shopping online?
   A it's much cheaper
   B there is less travelling involved
   C payment time is much quicker
   D there are more choices
3 What does the author say you can do to make sure the connection is safe?
   A go to a website where you can check the address
   B contact the website by sending them a message
   C look for a special icon on the screen
   D look for the word 'secure' in the website address

4 According to the author, why is it important to create a strong password?
   A so only you and the shop know your password
   B so no one can guess your password and see everything you do
   C so you can shop happily online with no worries
   D so only you and the bank know your password
5 Why does the author suggest you check other customers' comments?
   A so we can see if the seller is honest
   B because they explain everything about the product
   C because the seller might not tell the truth about the product
   D so we can talk to them about the product or seller

3 Match the highlighted words in the text to their meanings.

1 when you want to and when you have time to
2 someone who sells something
3 the thing that you use when you close a door, window, etc. that needs a key to open it
4 more than 'quite', but less than 'very'

....
....
....
....

1 Write the past participle of these irregular verbs.

1 sing ....

2 make ....

3 steal ....

4 see ....

5 go ....

6 spend ....

7 win ....

8 be ....

2 Write full sentences, using the present perfect.

1 I / write / a letter / the newspaper ....

2 Sam / lose / his wallet ....

3 Jayde / never / borrow / any money ....

4 Jan / never / use / credit card online ....

5 Louise / catch / a bad cold ....

6 you / ever / buy / shoes / from a second-hand shop? ....

3 Complete these sentences with the correct form of the verbs in brackets.

1 I .... that book about South America! Can you buy it for me? (never / read)

2 Mum .... this much food from the supermarket before. I don't think we can eat it all! (never / buy)

3 Have you .... that shirt that was too big for you? (take back)

4 Right! I .... enough money to get my new bike. I'm going to buy it! (save up)

5 My aunt .... for the change when she .... us money to buy sweets. She's so kind! (never / ask) / (give)

6 I .... online before. Can you show me how to do it? (never / shop)

4 Correct the mistakes in these sentences.

1 Have you sell it or not? ....

2 Have you ever meet a famous person? ....

3 Today I am very happy as I have receive my new computer game. ....

4 I have pay for all our tickets to see the football match. ....

5 The shop assistant have charge me too much money! ....

The past participle of *go*: *been* and *gone*

5 Choose the correct answer.

1 Jake isn't here. He's *been* / *gone* home.

2 Where's Maggie? Has she *been* / *gone* to the library for the book club?

3 I haven't *been* / *gone* to your house.

4 We've *been* / *gone* to London many times.

5 Terese isn't here. She's *been* / *gone* to the shops.

6 Have you *been* / *gone* to the new sports club? It's amazing.

6 Complete the messages with either *been* or *gone*.

I've
1 ....
to the gym.
Back at 7 pm.

If you're reading
this, you've
2 ....
to the doctor's and
you're back! Call
them – you left your
bag there!

James has
3 ....
to the library for
you and collected
your books.
They're here.

Pip, we've
4 .... to
visit Grandma –
back later. Mum

VOCABULARY — Easily confused words: *pay, charge, cost*

1 Complete the sentences with the correct verb.

1 My new jeans _____ £45.
2 Can I _____ for this with my credit card?
3 They _____ £30 a year to be a member.

2 Complete the sentences with the correct form of the verbs in Exercise 1.

1 Entry is free. We aren't _____ anyone today.
2 It _____ £250 to fly to Prague.
3 Have you _____ for the tickets?

WRITING — A story (2)

» See *Prepare to write* box, Student's Book, page 57.

1 Look at the picture and read the first sentence of the story. What do you think happens in the story?

2 Read the first few sentences of Ricardo's story and check your ideas.

Sometimes when you're not looking for something, that's when you find it!
I didn't set out to buy anything that day. I was in my local town centre, just walking around window shopping. I saw some nice clothes and some beautiful art. Then I saw a really cool laptop, but it was quite expensive. Later I went to a cashpoint to see if I had any money, but I only had £30 in my bank account. It wasn't enough money to buy any of the things, so I took out the money and then kept on walking.
While I was waiting for the bus, suddenly I spotted something in the window of a technology store that I had often thought about buying – a wireless speaker for my smartphone. I have never been that lucky with sales, so I was amazed when I saw the price. It was reduced from £150 to £25. With £30 in my pocket, I don't think I've been so excited about a special offer in all my life! I raced into the shop and bought the speaker.
As soon as I arrived home, I ran upstairs to my room, connected my phone to the speaker and played my favourite songs. Life is full of surprises!

3 Read the *Prepare to write* box on Student's Book, page 57. Then read Ricardo's story again. Does it have a clear beginning, middle and end?

4 Look at the highlighted verbs in Ricardo's story. Match them to the simple verbs below.

1 ran _____
2 saw _____
3 started a journey _____
4 very surprised _____

5 Find five time adverbs and phrases in Ricardo's story. Then choose the correct time adverbs in the sentences.

1 I called the police *as soon as / while* I knew the man had stolen the car.
2 About six hours *then / later*, they found my dog in the park.
3 I *suddenly / when* saw a man running away.
4 I was watching a film *then / while* my mum read a book.

6 Read the task and plan your story.

- Your English teacher has asked you to write a story.
- Your story must begin with this sentence: *Jonathan stopped at his favourite shop and went inside.*
- Write your story.

7 Write your story.

- Write about 100 words.
- Remember to check your spelling and grammar.

VOCABULARY Food and drink adjectives

1 Find the food adjectives.

lionjuicysourhappydeliciousrawneverdisgustingspicybitteraprilhorriblesweetfrozencartastyfresh

2 Write the words from Exercise 1 next to their meanings.

1 full of juice
2 extremely pleasant to eat
3 produced or collected recently
4 with a taste or smell like a lemon
5 a strong taste that is not sweet
6 containing ingredients with a strong, hot flavour
7 extremely bad to taste
8 kept at a very low temperature
9 with a taste like sugar
10 pleasant to taste
11 not cooked
12 very unpleasant

3 Choose the correct adjective.

1 Valentina likes eating curries that are hot and *bitter / spicy / fresh*.
2 Marco and Lucia have bought some *frozen / fresh / bitter* vegetables from the market.
3 Sashimi isn't cooked – it's served *sour / raw / frozen*.
4 Dad made some lemon juice. It's really *sweet / sour / spicy*!
5 This pineapple is really *juicy / frozen / bitter*. It's from Barbados.
6 Mum gets cakes from the baker's every day. They're really *sweet / spicy / juicy*.
7 They keep the pizzas in the *sour / frozen / raw* section in the supermarket.
8 You need some sugar to eat grapefruit, otherwise it tastes a bit *juicy / bitter / sweet*.

4 Complete the sentences with adjectives from the box.

delicious	disgusting	horrible	tasty

1 Mmm, this chocolate cake is the best I've ever tasted! It's _____!
2 I don't enjoy eating chicken nuggets. They're really unhealthy and _____.
3 How can anyone eat insects? Ugh, they're _____!
4 I like eating lasagne. It's nice and _____.

READING

1 Which of the following fruits come from the hottest parts of the world? Which are from cooler parts?

| apple | banana | mango | pear | pineapple | strawberry |

Hotter	Cooler

2 Read Marta's blog and put the events in order. Write the numbers 1–6.

a Her parents decided to visit a farm. ....

b Marta wrote her blog post. ....

c Her parents' friends arrived from another country. ....

d They went on a tour of the farm. ....

e Marta took her school books with her. ....

f A man offered Marta a strange piece of fruit. ....

ABOUT • RECENT POSTS • SEND A MESSAGE • RECOMMENDATIONS

Hi guys! Just wanted to tell you what I've done recently. Well, we had some visitors from the UK and so Mum and Dad thought it would be nice to take them to Tropical Fruit World. They said, 'We haven't been, so let's go together. It looks interesting.' I know, it sounds so dull! I don't know how anyone could think it's interesting to go to a fruit farm! Anyhow, I had to go, so I took my music and books for some schoolwork and planned to have a drink in the café.

We got there and there weren't many people, and there were all these strange-looking fruits. A man asked me if I wanted to try some chocolate pudding fruit! I was like, 'What is that!?' I tried it and it really tasted like chocolate pudding. Then we tried others including jackfruit, which tastes like pineapple and banana together, and dragon fruit, which has a sweet taste. It's a bit odd but really delicious. There's also a chewing gum fruit, star apples and many more! It was so interesting – I had no idea.

Then we went on a walk with a woman from the farm, Betty. She showed us 50 different kinds of mango! I honestly thought there was just one variety of mango! Not true! Betty told us about many other amazing fruits too. Finally, we went to the café and tried some of them. In the end, I have to say it was a real adventure, and I was really pleased I went!

#fruit #thanks #mumanddad #parentsknowbest

3 Read Marta's blog again and choose the correct answer.

1 Marta visited the fruit farm *with her parents / on her own*.

2 Marta planned to *do her homework / sit in the car* while her parents were visiting the fruit farm.

3 When they arrived at the farm, they tried some fruits *they didn't know / that were familiar to them*.

4 Marta thought all the new fruit was *disgusting / tasty*.

5 Before Marta went to the farm, she *knew / didn't realise* that there were so many different types of mango.

6 By the end of her blog entry, Marta is *positive / disappointed* about the fruit farm.

4 Complete the sentences with the highlighted words from the text.

1 I .... bought some tropical fruits in the supermarket.

2 This book is really .... – nothing exciting happens.

3 Mum usually makes a .... for Sunday lunch.

4 You can buy a .... of teas from the new tea shop that's opened in town.

5 Look at this .... message I've received. Do you understand it?

GRAMMAR — Present perfect and past simple; *How long?* and *for/since*

1 Complete the sentences with the correct form of the verbs in brackets.

1 Frank _____ in a restaurant since he was 18 years old. (work)
2 I _____ sushi many times. (eat)
3 Mum _____ an amazing meal for my birthday tomorrow. (prepare)
4 Anja _____ me to her party night next week. (not invite)
5 My mum _____ Chinese food for the first time last week – it was delicious! (cook)
6 Perry and Max really _____ the food at Café Domu last night. They thought it was disgusting! (not like)
7 How long _____ Uncle Tim in New York? (live)
8 I _____ spicy curry for about ten years. (love)
9 Mum and Dad _____ with Auntie Betty when they were in London last week. (stay)
10 _____ you _____ this new pasta meal? It's so tasty! (try)

2 Complete the sentences with *for* or *since*.

1 The new chef has been there _____ about three months now.
2 Christine has cooked the family's Sunday lunch _____ she was 12 years old.
3 Pete has known his best friend, Joe, _____ he joined the club.
4 I've had this apple in my bag _____ ages. I need to eat it quick!
5 The boys have been waiting here _____ 20 minutes.
6 I haven't been to my favourite restaurant _____ my last birthday.
7 I've known my best friend _____ five years.
8 We haven't had pasta for dinner _____ last month.
9 My aunt has been in India _____ three months.
10 I haven't had a really tasty burger _____ the one I had in New Orleans last year.

3 Complete the text with the correct form of the verbs in brackets.

A Bassington restaurant owner was surprised on Saturday when the famous chef Zaza Gabon [1] _____ (walk) in for dinner. Bruno Aires, the owner, [2] _____ (say), 'She [3] _____ (come) in at about 8 pm with another lady who I [4] _____ (see) around Bassington quite often. They [5] _____ (eat) fish and chips.' Zaza Gabon [6] _____ (write) many cook books and [7] _____ (appear) on TV shows. She [8] _____ (live) in South Africa for the first 20 years of her life until she [9] _____ (meet) the film star Josh Henderson. They [10] _____ (live) in the UK since 2012.

4 Choose the correct sentence in each pair.

👁 1 a Since I saw the film, I wanted it.
 b Since I saw the film, I have wanted it.
2 a I've known him for two years.
 b I've known him since two years.
3 a I received your letter yesterday.
 b I've received your letter yesterday.
4 a I haven't talked to you since years!
 b I haven't talked to you for years!
5 a How long have you know your friend?
 b How long have you known your friend?

VOCABULARY — *look, taste, smell*

1 Complete the sentences with the correct form of *look*, *taste* or *smell*.

1 That apple pie _____ tasty. I like the way you have put apples on the top too.
2 I'm not sure I can eat all of this meal. It _____ horrible!
3 This peach _____ delicious. Would you like one?
4 This milk _____ a bit sour. I don't think I'll drink it.
5 Dinner _____ really spicy – what are we having?
6 The sashimi in the restaurant window _____ so fresh! Let's go there next week!

2 Complete the conversation with the correct form of *look*, *taste* or *smell*.

A: I went to the new restaurant in town last night. It was good.
B: It always [1] _____ nice in there. What did you have?
A: An amazing Thai curry which [2] _____ beautiful and [3] _____ delicious.
B: Did you have a dessert?
A: I did. It was a cake and I didn't know what was in it, but I thought I could [4] _____ coconut – and when I [5] _____ it, I was right!
B: It sounds great – maybe we should go there together.
A: Good idea!

1 Look at the pictures in Exercise 2. What can you see in each picture?

2 You are going to listen to some short extracts. For each question, choose the correct answer.
08

1 What did the girl most enjoy eating when she went to Brazil?

A

B

C

2 Where is the boy going to have lunch?

A

B

C

3 What does the girl usually eat for breakfast?

A

B

C

4 Which dish is the girl's father going to cook?

A

B

C

5 What did the boy have a problem making?

A

B

C

6 Where did the man get his recipe from?

A

B

C

7 Who does the girl think should win the cookery competition?

A

B

C

3 Listen again and check your answers.
08

11 A HEALTHY FUTURE

VOCABULARY Body and health

1 Write the letters in the correct order to make words and label the body.

nich
lewbo
gnierf
nalek
cabk
deshoulr
neke
sehct
rothat
bmtuh
rofedeah
teo

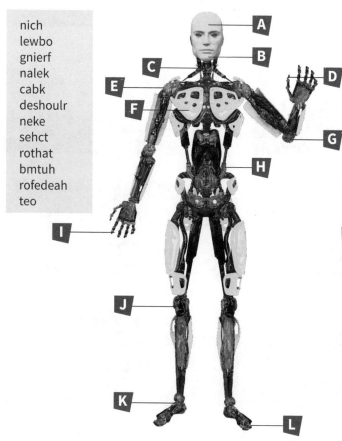

2 Choose the correct word.

1 I can hardly speak – my *neck / throat* really hurts.
2 I fell and hurt my *thumb / ankle* and now I can't walk.
3 Ibrahim fell on his face in the playground and cut his *toe / chin*.
4 Dad fell off his horse and hurt his *shoulder / forehead*. He can't move his arm very well.
5 Billy is always falling over and hurting his *throat / knees*.
6 Mary can't play the piano because she has injured her *finger / toe*.
7 My brother's broken his *thumb / throat*, so he can't play tennis today.
8 I didn't see the shelf and I walked straight into it. I've cut my *forehead / elbow*.
9 I have to go to the dentist because I have *stomach ache / toothache*.
10 I have a bad *chin / cough* – but the medicine tastes disgusting!
11 She had a pain in her *chest / cough* and so she went to hospital.
12 I have to stay in bed for a week to rest my *cold / back*.

3 Match the sentence halves.

1 I've got   a a bone.
2 My throat is   b on my finger.
3 I've got a high   c sore.
4 I've got a cut   d fever.
5 My legs   e a bad cold.
6 Julie broke   f ache.

4 Complete the text with the words in the box.

ache   earache   fever
flu   headache   temperature
toothache   throat

Last year I had a maths test and I hadn't studied, so I didn't want to go to school. I told my mum that my mouth was hurting. 'Mum, I've got [1]_____. I don't think I can go to school.' She said, 'Get up and have your breakfast.' I put my hands over my ears. 'Mum, I've got really bad [2]_____ too.' 'Eat your breakfast,' she said. 'You might feel better after breakfast.' But I didn't eat anything. 'My arms and legs [3]_____, Mum, and my [4]_____ is sore. I've got a [5]_____.' I held my head in my hands as I spoke. 'I think I've got [6]_____, Mum. I feel awful! I don't think I can go to school today.' She said, 'Hmm, OK, let's go to the doctor's.' So we went to the doctor's. He examined me and took my [7]_____. Then he said to my mum, 'Tom has a really high [8]_____. His temperature is 39°C. Give him this medicine and make sure that he stays in bed for a week. No computers, no books and no TV. Just rest.' I didn't understand – I mean, I wasn't really ill!

1 Read the article quickly and tick (✓) the ideas that are mentioned.

1 what to do if you hurt yourself ☐
2 taking the right medicines ☐
3 preparing your body before you exercise ☐

4 how important your mind is ☐
5 eating the right foods ☐
6 getting into good habits when you are young ☐

TEENAGE MAG
ABOUT   WHAT'S NEW   CONTACT US

BODY AND MIND

Everybody knows that exercise is good for you. But what about exercise for the mind – how can that help you? *Teenage Mag* **spoke to Dr Bathurst, a yoga teacher, about the benefits of yoga.**

TM: Many people think that yoga is a slow, boring activity. Tell us why it isn't.

DR B: Well, yoga is about body and mind. Your mind and your body are working together, and it can be quite fast too. You can't always see that though. You stretch your body – you know, make it longer – and you do the same with your mind. In yoga, you have to get your body into some difficult positions, for example, standing on one foot and moving your whole body forward. Your mind can help you do this. If you look at one place and just think about that, then it's easier. This is something you can learn to do. For young people who enjoy sport, yoga can help them think – you know, concentrate. In football, for example, people are always shouting at you and telling you what to do. If you can concentrate, then you have a better chance of scoring a goal. Yoga can help with concentration for your school studies too.

TM: And can it help if you're ill? If you break your arm, or if you get toothache?

DR B: Well, then you have to go to the doctor or the dentist, but if you know how to take it easy, you'll get better faster.

TM: And yoga can help you avoid some injuries, can't it?

DR B: Yes. That's perhaps more important with older people, but it's good to get used to stretching when you're younger. Before you exercise, you should always warm up. This is so that your body is warm and you can stretch more without hurting yourself.

TM: Thank you very much! Here at *Teenage Mag* we're all going to try out a yoga class.

COMMENTS

I love yoga, or any of these kinds of activities. It's really important to be able to concentrate.
Celine, Switzerland

My basketball coach makes us do warm-up exercises before we have a match. He always shouts out 'You'll play better if you stretch!' Now I understand why!
Diego, Argentina

This is true. My friend injured her ankle and the doctor said that it was because she hadn't warmed up properly.
Itzel, Mexico

2 Read the article again and choose the correct word.

1 Dr Bathurst is a *yoga instructor / dentist*.
2 Yoga is *not as slow as / slower than* people think, according to Dr Bathurst.
3 He says people who do yoga *learn how to concentrate / are good at sports*.
4 People who do yoga may *get well sooner / take longer to get well* than people who don't.
5 Yoga can help you because you *prepare your body / test your body* for activity.

3 Who mentions these things in the comments? Write *Celine*, *Diego* or *Itzel*.

1 something that happened to somebody else ....
2 preparing for sport by exercising first ....
3 enjoying activities that are similar to yoga ....

4 Match the highlighted words in the article to the meanings.

1 get used to ....
2 stretch ....
3 take it easy ....
4 avoid ....
5 warm up ....

a make your body, or part of your body, longer and straighter
b relax and not worry about something
c get to know something so it is no longer unusual
d do gentle exercise to prepare for harder exercise
e stop something from happening

GRAMMAR *will* and *be going to*

1 Write the words in the correct order to make sentences.

1 We're / later / to / dinner / going / have / together

2 going / to / Josie's / her / in / grandma / hospital / visit / after school

3 will/ teacher / give / our / a tennis lesson / us / today / I hope

4 she'll / Mum / up / pick us / football practice / after / says

5 operation / leg / to / an / is / have / her / on / Stephanie / going

6 in here / hot / the window / a bit / I'll / open / It's / so

7 party / I'll / some / I think / to / your / pizza / bring

8 a / competition / are / to / All the boys / enter / going

2 Complete the conversation with the correct form of *will* or *be going to*.

Mrs Jones: Edite, we [1] .... take you to hospital. Then a doctor can look at your knee.

Edite: Who [2] .... take me, Mrs Jones?

Mrs Jones: I can, but would you like a friend to come too?

Edite: Yes, please. My brother, Rufus. I'm sure he [3] .... want to come.

Mrs Jones: OK, I [4] .... go and fetch him from class. Oh, look, there's Maisie!

Maisie: Hi, Mrs Jones. Edite, are you OK?

Edite: I fell over and Mrs Jones [5] .... take me to hospital. Maisie, can you get Rufus, please?

Maisie: Sure, I [6] .... text him now. And I [7] .... pick up all your things.

Edite: Thanks, Maisie. I [8] .... miss our English lesson – can you take notes, please?

Maisie: Sure!

Mrs Jones: Don't worry, Edite, you [9] .... be fine.

3 Complete the short conversations with the correct form of *will* or *be going to*.

A: When [1] .... (you/do) your homework?

B: I [2] .... (do) it after dinner.

A: Your phone's ringing. Would you like me to get it for you?

B: No, it's OK. I [3] .... (not/answer) it now. I [4] .... (check) it later.

A: Bobbie [5] .... (have) a birthday party. [6] .... (you/go)?

B: I don't know. I think I [7] .... (stay) at home and watch TV.

A: [8] .... (help) me with my homework, Mum?

B: I can't, but your dad [9] .... (explain) it to you. He loved maths when he was a child!

4 Complete the conversation with the correct form of the verbs in the box. Use *will* or *be going to*.

| ask | be | drive | get |
| go | look | stay | take |

Sasha is at home with a fever. Her mum is talking to her.

'OK, I [1] .... you to the doctor's this morning.'

'Oh, really, Mum. I'm sure it [2] .... away soon.'

'No, I've decided. The doctor [3] .... at you and make sure it's nothing serious. I [4] .... some medicine for your cough, Sasha.'

'Urgh! I hate that medicine! It tastes disgusting!'

'I know, but I want you to get better.'

'OK, Mum. But I [5] .... in bed. I feel ill.'

'I know, but the doctor can't give you medicine without seeing you. I [6] .... my car keys and we [7] .... in now. I don't think it [8] .... very busy now.'

5 Correct the mistakes in these sentences or tick (✓) any you think are correct.

1 I will be send you a message tonight.

2 I know we're going to have an awesome time!

3 We will looking at the map tomorrow and decide where to go.

4 I enjoy spending time with her because they're moments that are will not happened again.

5 My friends and I talk a lot about what we'll do in the future.

VOCABULARY | Illnesses and injuries: verbs

1 Choose the correct verb.

1 Fran *caught* / *broke* a really bad cold recently.
2 I can't concentrate. My head *hurts* / *feels*.
3 Maggie fell off her bike and *had* / *broke* her arm.
4 The athlete has *injured* / *got* his knee, so he can't take part in the race.
5 The little boy fell over and *felt* / *cut* both of his elbows.
6 Are you *feeling* / *getting* OK? Sit down here.

2 Complete the text with the correct form of the verbs in the box. Use each verb once.

be	break	catch	cut	feel
get	have	hurt	injure	

Something ¹_____ wrong with everyone in my class at the moment! Jessica fell over in basketball and ²_____ her knee. She can walk, but it really ³_____. Unfortunately, Sam wasn't so lucky. He also fell over and he has ⁴_____ his arm. Mary isn't at school because she ⁵_____ flu. We think she ⁶_____ it from Fred, who came back to school yesterday. Monica was cooking something last week and she ⁷_____ her finger with a knife. I hope everyone ⁸_____ better soon, but I don't ⁹_____ very well myself!

WRITING | An article (1)

>> See *Prepare to write*, Student's Book, page 67.

1 What are the benefits of keeping fit?

2 Read the notice. What does the article have to be about? What suggestions would you make?

You see the following notice in a magazine:

ARTICLES WANTED!

There are lots of benefits to keeping fit. Many people don't realise the number of ways it can improve your quality of life. How can it improve your school life? How can it improve your personal life? How can it improve your social life?

Write an article answering these three questions and we will publish the most interesting articles in our magazine.

3 Read the article. (The parts are not in the correct order.) Does it include any of your ideas?

A To sum up, keeping fit isn't only good for our health, it can also improve our quality of life.

B Many people think that keeping fit is only important for our health. However, it also has other important benefits.

C First of all, after doing physical exercise we feel calmer and happier, and this feels like a reward for working so hard. Secondly, we're also more sociable because we meet new people when we play sport. It can also help you in your educational lives because when you play a sport, it improves your ability to concentrate, which helps you work better.

4 Match the parts of the article 1–3 with paragraphs A–C in Exercise 3.

1 Introduction _____
2 Main article _____
3 Conclusion _____

5 Read the article in the correct order. Then choose the best title.

1 How to be fit and healthy
2 The benefits of keeping fit
3 The best reasons to keep fit

6 Read the notice. What does the article need to be about? Make notes of your suggestions.

You see this notice in a magazine:

ARTICLES WANTED!

There are lots of sports to choose from to help us keep fit. Which sport helps you to keep healthy and fit? What do you like about the sport? How does it make you fitter?

7 Write your article.

- Use your notes from Exercise 6.
- Remember to check your spelling and grammar.
- Use the structure and suggestions from the *Prepare to write* box.
- Write about 100 words.

VOCABULARY Animals

1 Add the missing letters (a, e, i, o, u, y) to complete these animal words.

1 f l __
2 b __ t
3 w __ r m
4 s h __ r k
5 __ n t
6 w __ l f
7 f __ x
8 b __ t t __ r f l __
9 f r __ g
10 m __ s q __ __ t __
11 d __ n k __ y
12 d __ __ r
13 b __ __
14 __ __ g l __

2 Complete the puzzle and find the hidden animal.

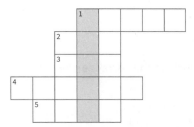

Which animal

1 lives in the ocean and has very sharp teeth?
2 is very small and can be black or red?
3 is small and flies at night?
4 is like a small horse?
5 is quite big and lives in the forest?

Hidden word: ....

3 Read these descriptions. Which animal is it?

1 ....
I've always loved these animals – they're similar to dogs. They hunt in groups called packs and are very intelligent. They live in forests and deserts but also in mountains and even in cold regions of the Arctic. They communicate with each other by making a long sad sound, called a howl, that can be heard as far as 10–16 kilometres away.

2 ....
These animals are usually small and green but can be different colours. They are born in water and then live in the water or on the land. They can be found all over the world. They are fantastic jumpers.

3 ....
These insects are often really pretty. They have beautiful wings, but they cannot fly if their body temperature is less than 30 °C. So you won't see them on cold days!

4 ....
These birds are some of the largest in the world. They have amazing eyesight and can see things from up to three kilometres away. They fly very high in the sky and they kill smaller animals for food.

5 ....
It's not often you see these animals because they are very quiet. Unlike dogs or wolves, they don't hunt in groups; they do this alone and usually at night. They are very clever and have incredible hearing – they can hear mice underground.

6 ....
You can see these animals every day in your garden or in fields or parks. They are long and thin and don't have any arms or legs. They mostly live in the earth.

4 Match the animals in Exercise 3 to the pictures.

1 ....   3 ....   5 ....
2 ....   4 ....   6 ....

1 What do you think 'native animal' means? Read the article quickly to find out.

1 an animal that is from a certain part of the world
2 an animal that lives in many different places
3 an animal that stays in the same place all its life

2 Read the article and choose the correct answer, A, B, C or D.

1 What is the writer doing in this article?
   A complaining about a wildlife organisation
   B describing what a wildlife organisation does
   C reporting an interview with an animal expert
   D giving advice about how to look after pets
2 What does the writer say about WIRES?
   A The courses they provide are rather disappointing.
   B The visits they make to farms in the area are helpful.
   C They should explain how they look after the animals.
   D They are doing a very important job in Australia.
3 What does Guy's dad do for the organisation?
   A He tries to save animals that are hurt.
   B He answers the phone at the WIRES office.
   C He chooses someone to go and see the animal.
   D He prepares the special clothes for WIRES helpers.
4 What happened to the baby bat?
   A It was injured by other bats.
   B It is now looked after by Guy at home.
   C It lived and was put back into the wild.
   D It is still living at the animal centre.
5 What would someone working for WIRES say?
   A We can send someone out quickly to help your pet in your home or farm.
   B If you see a snake, a bat or another wild animal in danger, call us immediately.
   C We are a new organisation in Australia that looks after all kinds of animals.
   D If you want to have a career with us, you must attend at least one of our courses.

3 Match the highlighted words in the article to their meanings.

1 look after someone or something ....
2 become involved in doing an activity with a group of people ....
3 save someone or something from a dangerous situation ....
4 arrange and run an event ....

This month Angelina Horsefield writes about an animal rescue organisation in Australia:

WIRES

WIRES (Wildlife Information and Rescue Service) began in 1985 when someone found an injured bird in a park in Sydney, Australia. At the time, no one knew how to help this 'native' animal. WIRES helps animals like snakes, kangaroos and, of course, birds. However, they can only help native Australian wildlife – animals that originally come from Australia. That means they can't help other animals like cats or rabbits that were brought to Australia from other parts of the world.

Like other animal rescue groups, WIRES needs more people. I believe they are definitely helping the local animals, but they can only continue if others join in. They hold excellent courses, where people can learn what to do when they find an injured animal. They also explain what happens to the animals in their care. Many of the people who help also take care of the animals themselves in their own gardens or on their farms.

I spoke to 15-year-old Guy McKenzie, whose dad helps WIRES in his free time. Guy told me about the work they do. 'Dad usually gets a phone call at home and drives immediately to where the animal is, to rescue it. He has special equipment and always wears gloves. The animals are wild, after all!'

Guy also talked about a woman who found a bat in her garden. She thought it might be dead, but then she noticed that there was a baby bat too. Guy's dad brought it back to the centre, where it grew into a healthy adult. Then, WIRES was able to return it to nature. Guy showed me a baby kangaroo that his dad was looking after and told me that one day he'll be doing the same thing. Yes, he will, for sure.

READ MORE

GRAMMAR Modals of probability

1 Complete the conversation with *might*, *must*, *can't* or *could*.

A: What's that? Oh, I know, it ¹_____ be a big cat.

B: Mm, I don't think so. It ²_____ be an elephant because it's too small.

A: Right, but it's an African animal. It ³_____ be a rhino but it's the wrong colour.

B: I know! It ⁴_____ be a giraffe – look at its skin!

2 Choose the correct answer.

1 I _____ watch a programme about animals tonight.
   a might **b** can't
2 That _____ be the longest snake I've ever seen!
   a can't **b** must
3 Phil _____ be ill because he isn't at school today.
   a might **b** can't
4 It _____ be a parrot. It's the wrong colour!
   a can't **b** must
5 I know you've lost your book. _____ this be it?
   a Can't **b** Could
6 You _____ be really excited – you have tickets for your favourite band!
   a must **b** could
7 Taylor _____ call me later, but she's not sure.
   a must **b** might
8 I'm tired. It _____ be time for bed.
   a must **b** can't

3 Complete the sentences with the correct modal verb. Sometimes more than one answer is possible.

1 I think it _____ rain today – look at the sky.
2 This _____ be for me – I don't like nature magazines.
3 You _____ be really happy with your new pet dog!
4 That animal _____ bite you – watch out!
5 It looks like a dog, but it lives in the forest. It _____ be a wolf.
6 Everyone's wearing hats and coats. It _____ be very cold.
7 I can't find my books, but they _____ be at school.
8 It _____ be a fox. It's the size of a small horse!

4 Complete the sentences with the correct modal verb. Sometimes more than one answer is possible.

A: What are you reading? And what is that?

B: It's an amazing animal. It ¹_____ be very clever to do the things it does.

A: Right! It ²_____ be from Europe! Look at those trees and the background!

B: No, I think it ³_____ be from South America somewhere. I haven't finished reading it yet!

A: Well, I ⁴_____ do my 'wonderful animals' project about this! Can I have the magazine?

5 Choose the correct sentence in each pair.

1 **a** I think this can be difficult to do.
   b I think this might be difficult to do.
2 **a** They must be beautiful!
   b They might to be beautiful!
3 **a** I thought that you might want to come to my house to play the game with me.
   b I thought that you want to come to my house to play the game with me.
4 **a** She's smiling. She must be so pleased with her new pet rabbit.
   b She's smiling. She can't be pleased with her new pet rabbit
5 **a** I thought that the exhibition about the future of your city must be very interesting.
   b I thought that the exhibition about the future of your city might be very interesting.
6 **a** There's a new job available at the café. It could be just what you're looking for.
   b There's a new job available at the café. It must be just what you're looking for.

1 Write the words in the correct order to make sentences.

1 is / This / not / definitely / cat / my

....

2 your brother / Perhaps / help / with / your work / can / you

....

3 probably / a / That / famous painting / is / very

....

4 probably / to / tomorrow / the dolphins / going / We're / see

....

5 phone / definitely / are / Mum and Dad / buy / going to / another / me / not

....

6 perhaps / I'm / certain / zoo / opens / not / but / summer / in / the / the

....

2 Choose the correct words to complete the text.

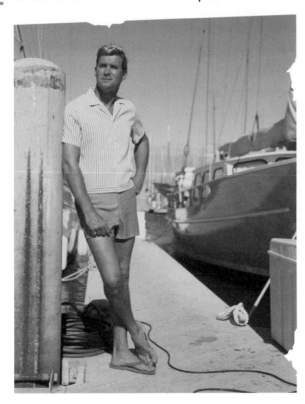

| definitely | definitely not |
| perhaps | probably |

This is an old photo I found in the attic. I showed it to my mum, but she doesn't know much about it. Judging by the clothes, she thinks it's
¹ .... from the 1960s, but she isn't sure. She says it's ² .... my grandfather because that's just what he looked like when she was a little girl. He looks young in the photo, so ³ .... it was before he married my grandmother. It's ⁴ .... after I was born because he didn't have any hair then!

1 You are going to hear a girl called Kate talking about a story she wrote for a competition. Tick (✓) the questions you think you will hear.

1 What's your full name? ☐
2 Can you tell us something about your story? ☐
3 Why did you write about fish? ☐
4 What's your favourite animal? ☐
5 Why did you enter the competition? ☐

 2 Listen and check your answers.

 3 Listen again and choose the correct answer.

1 What is Kate's story about?
  a why a boy and his parents moved to London
  b how a teenage boy enjoys being with his animals
2 Kate wrote about fish because
  a they are her favourite animals.
  b she looks after some for her mother.
3 Why did Kate enter the competition?
  a Her teacher asked her to.
  b She wanted a new challenge.
4 Marco is
  a an unhappy boy.
  b a boy who enjoys fishing.
5 What does Kate do to relax?
  a She writes more stories.
  b She spends time in the countryside.

4 The picture is about Kate's story. Tick (✓) the sentences that are correct.

1 I can see a boy. He's looking at a fish. ☐
2 There's a window in the background and we can see the countryside. ☐
3 There are three people in the picture and the one on the right is taking a picture. ☐
4 On the right there's a table and on the left there is a bookcase. ☐
5 The boy is probably looking at the fish because he likes it. ☐

13 MIXED FEELINGS

VOCABULARY — Adjectives: moods and feelings

1 Find 12 adjectives in the word square (→ ↓ ↘).

e	d	t	f	h	c	r	s	y	o	r	i
x	n	e	b	e	o	u	t	p	l	h	q
h	a	u	t	b	n	p	r	o	p	q	r
a	m	m	h	q	f	x	e	c	r	y	e
u	y	f	a	n	u	n	s	f	o	m	l
s	l	f	z	s	q	s	n	u	s	a	
t	b	r	a	v	e	l	e	i	d	l	x
e	d	x	c	r	d	d	d	g	f	d	e
d	i	s	a	p	p	o	i	n	t	e	d
e	m	b	a	r	r	a	s	s	e	d	f
o	x	h	g	r	a	t	e	f	u	l	a
s	c	a	r	e	d	r	d	h	w	n	l

2 Write the words from the word square next to their meanings.

1 extremely surprised
2 feeling very pleased about something you have done
3 showing thanks for something
4 not able to think clearly or to understand something
5 thinking something positive will happen
6 unhappy because someone or something was not as good as you hoped
7 very tired
8 not frightened in dangerous or difficult situations
9 feeling happy because nothing is worrying you
10 frightened something bad will happen
11 worried and not able to relax
12 feeling ashamed or shy

3 Complete the sentences with the adjectives from the box. There is one adjective you don't need.

> amazed   confused   disappointed
> embarrassed   exhausted
> grateful   hopeful   proud
> relaxed   scared   stressed

1 Danny is _____ that he won't pass the exam – he hasn't studied very hard.
2 I don't understand what you're saying – I'm _____.
3 Alison didn't get what she wanted for her birthday. She's a bit _____.
4 Jack does yoga because it makes him feel _____.
5 I'm so _____ of our school – we won the competition.
6 I don't know how I got 100% in my maths exam. I'm _____!
7 Pedro felt _____ when he had to speak in front of the whole class.
8 Eva is _____ that she will win the swimming race.
9 I've been running for half an hour and now I feel completely _____!
10 Carol is feeling _____ because she has a test tomorrow and she's working hard.

4 Choose the two words that best describe the people in each situation.

1 Emma usually gets the best marks in class and she will be very surprised if she isn't top of the class again. She's never worried before an exam.
   a amazed   **b** scared   **c** relaxed
2 Mrs Paderewski has worked many hours recently. She bought a new computer and she went on an expensive holiday, but now she feels worried and can't relax.
   a embarrassed   **b** exhausted   **c** stressed
3 Jackson is very pleased that his team played so well and they won the match. He is unhappy that he didn't score a goal though.
   a grateful   **b** proud   **c** disappointed
4 We sometimes do quizzes at home and I don't always know the answers to even simple questions. My face goes red! Last night we played and there was so much noise I couldn't think properly.
   a embarrassed   **b** hopeful   **c** confused
5 Jan has passed all his exams and now feels happy and calm. His parents are very pleased, too, and have organised a big party at their house.
   a proud   **b** relaxed   **c** brave

THE WORLD'S COOLEST MARATHON

1 You are going to read an article about the North Pole Marathon. Tick (✓) the ideas that you think will be mentioned.

1 how many people have run the North Pole Marathon ☐
2 which country the marathon takes place in ☐
3 what motivates some people to do the marathon ☐
4 the amount of time it takes to complete the marathon ☐
5 how long it takes to train for the marathon ☐
6 how much it costs to enter the marathon ☐

2 Read the article quickly and check your answers.

If you think running a marathon is difficult enough, you'd be amazed at the brave athletes who complete the North Pole Marathon. Wearing extra-warm clothes, they have to deal with heavy snow and temperatures of −30 °C to complete the 49-kilometre race. Although marathons take place all over the world, this particular marathon is the only one that's entirely on 'water'. **(1)** _____ That is the only time when the whole course becomes solid ice, giving the hopeful runners the best chance of finishing the race.

Since the annual event started in 2003, 480 people from around the world have successfully completed the race. Stefanie Pettersson from Brazil is one of the youngest people to achieve this. She was just 16 years and two weeks old on the day of the race. **(2)** _____ An experienced runner, Anders Pettersson encouraged Stefanie not to give up when she felt too cold or exhausted to continue. Another competitor who ran with Stefanie and Anders was Ted Jackson from the UK. He took up running when his father and brother developed health problems. **(3)** _____ To avoid that situation, he decided to get really fit.

How long does this marathon take? The men's record is 3 hours 36 minutes, and the women's is 4 hours 52 minutes. Runners have sometimes said they felt disappointed with their finishing times because they have run much faster in other marathons. But it's never possible to predict how well someone is going to do. **(4)** _____

Many of those who run the North Pole Marathon are trying to raise money for various charities. They collect money from friends and family by advertising what they plan to do. **(5)** _____ They are grateful for everything they receive because the entry fee alone is £16,000. This does, however, include all flights, accommodation and medical support.

3 Five sentences have been removed from the text. For each question, choose the correct answer (A–H). There are three extra sentences which you do not need to use.

A Neither of them actually expected to finish it.
B He was scared the same thing might happen to him.
C The difficult conditions meant he never felt relaxed.
D This could be on the internet or local TV.
E The darkness made them feel confused and stressed.
F For obvious reasons, it can only be attempted during winter.
G Weather conditions vary so much from year to year.
H Her dad was also one of the competitors.

4 Match the highlighted words in the article with their meanings.

1 the best or fastest ever
2 the money you pay to join an organisation, go into a place or take part in something
3 happening once a year
4 said good things to someone to make them confident about doing something
5 official organisations that give money, food or help to people who need it

GRAMMAR · *just, already* and *yet*

1 **Write the words in the correct order to make sentences.**

1 hasn't / The / yet / started / film

2 has / photos / just / uploaded / Shelly / the

3 finished / He's / game / that / already

4 out / have / Dad / gone / and / just / Mum

5 already / my / I've / done / homework

6 go / to / I'm / ready / yet / not / out

2 **Match the questions to the answers.**

1 Have you finished that work already?
2 Do I have to take my shoes off?
3 Do you want to go to the cinema?
4 Has anyone heard from Becky?
5 Have you managed to buy the tickets yet?
6 What's happened?

a No, I've already seen the film three times.
b Yes, I've just cleaned the floor!
c No, I think we're too late.
d My team has just lost. I'm so disappointed.
e Yes, it was really easy.
f No, not yet. I think she's stressed about her exams.

3 **Choose the correct words to complete the blog entry.**

Hi guys!!

I'm really proud of everyone. I've ¹*just / already* read the news on our social media page. It's great that we're having a party for the whole school. We've ²*already / yet* planned the food. I haven't looked at the replies to our invitations ³*yet / already*. But we're hopeful that loads of people are coming! Does anyone know why some of the kids in Mr Barker's class haven't received their invitations ⁴*yet / already*? Oh, it's OK! Eric Styles has ⁵*just / yet* emailed me to say he thinks there's an email problem with that class. He's going to re-send it.

Has anyone thought about the music ⁶*just / yet*? Let's talk about that at the next meeting. I've ⁷*yet / just* sent the people who are organising it a text message, so check your phones.

Tina K.

End-of-Year Party Club

4 **Complete the sentences with *just, already* or *yet*.**

1 I've _____ had dinner – about ten minutes ago!
2 I haven't finished reading that book _____ .
3 I'm so disappointed that my books haven't arrived _____ .
4 Mum said she has _____ sent a text. Check your phone.
5 Sally's _____ left for the library – Mum's taken her.
6 Mr Bentley has _____ said there's no homework this week! I'm so grateful!
7 I've _____ seen this film – I went with Barry last week.
8 Dad hasn't had his job interview _____ . He's hopeful he'll get the job.
9 The train has _____ left – right on time!
10 Have you been to the new sports centre _____ ? I went yesterday and it's really great!

5 **Correct the mistakes in these sentences or tick (✓) any you think are correct.**

1 I just have found a very interesting game online.

2 I haven't seen yet my new house.

3 I haven't already bought a book to take on holiday. What do you think I should take?

4 I have just got a new computer game.

5 We have already decided that you should bring a cake.

VOCABULARY · Adjectives: *-ed* or *-ing*

1 **Choose the correct adjective.**

1 Maggie is doing her homework and she's *bored / boring*.
2 I hate it when my mum asks me about school – it's so *annoying / annoyed*.
3 Dad felt *relaxing / relaxed* after playing his guitar.
4 It was *surprising / surprised* that Anne won the game so easily.
5 I'm a bit *confused / confusing* about the ending of the book – what actually happened?
6 Johnny stood up in class but forgot what to say – he was *embarrassing / embarrassed*.
7 We went to bed early last night because we were *tiring / tired*.
8 This new video game is *disappointing / disappointed*.
9 This film is really *bored / boring* – I think I'll read a book instead.
10 Were you *surprised / surprising* to hear that Joe won first prize in the competition?

2 Complete the sentences with the correct adjectives from the box.

> annoyed / annoying   bored / boring
> confused / confusing
> embarrassed / embarrassing

1 I really liked the first *Fast Cars* film, but I thought the second film, *Even Faster Cars*, was so _____. I actually fell asleep at one point.

2 I tried to explain to my dad how to use Snapchat, but he just looked really _____. I don't think he'll ever understand technology.

3 My sister is _____ with me at the moment because I borrowed her top without asking and got tomato ketchup on it.

4 The other day I called my teacher 'Mum' by mistake and everyone laughed at me. I was so _____!

WRITING   An article (2)

» See *Prepare to write* box, Student's Book, page 79.

1 You see this notice on an international English-language website. How do you think you can start your day positively?

> ### ARTICLES WANTED!
>
> How do you start your day in a positive way? Do you do any activities or have any routines in the morning to help you wake up? How do they make you feel?
>
> **Tell us what you think!**
>
> Write an article answering these questions.

2 Read the article below. Write notes of the answers to the questions in the notice.

> Are you one of those people who find it difficult to get up in the morning?
>
> People describe me as quite a positive person, but I'm not always like this when I get out of bed. So I find the best way to feel happy is to listen to music.
>
> I absolutely love music. When I wake up, it makes me feel more alive and it makes me want to move. Sometimes when I'm in the shower, I listen to something fast and energetic and do a little dance and sing. Other times I listen to something relaxing to stop me from feeling stressed. I sit quietly eating my breakfast and think about how I can make my day a positive one. For me, music is the best way to make my day a happier one!

3 Which of these phrases are used in the article?

Ask questions to get the reader's attention:
Have you ever …?
Are you one of those people who …?
Can you imagine …?
Make your article interesting:
I absolutely love music.
When I wake up, it makes me feel more alive.
It makes me want to move.
Give your own opinion:
I think …
For me, …
Speaking personally, …

4 Read the article notices below. Match each notice 1–3 to a question a–c that could begin the article.

> 1 How often do you feel proud? What makes you proud? And what do you do when you feel that way?

> 2 When was the last time you felt stressed? Why did you feel that way? And what did you do about it?

> 3 Are you the type of person who is relaxed when taking an exam? Why do you think you feel this way? Do you have any tips on how to stay relaxed?

a Are you one of those people who doesn't get stressed studying for tests? _____

b Have you ever felt really worried about doing something you knew you weren't that good at? _____

c Have you ever done something really well and felt very happy because of it? _____

5 Match two more possible sentences a–f to each notice 1–3 in Exercise 4.

a I just know in my heart when I can do something well.

b I usually go to my room when my mum and I have had an argument.

c I prepare well and never leave studying to the last minute.

d I just listen to music and it makes me feel better.

e I love studying in the night because it's the best time.

f I always stand up in class and give the teacher the right answer.

6 Write your article. You can use any of the notices on this page.

- Organise your article into paragraphs.
- Use phrases from the *Prepare to write* box.
- Remember to check your spelling and grammar.
- Write about 100 words.

14 ON SCREEN

VOCABULARY TV and film

1 Write the letters in the correct order to make film and TV genres.

1 rhoorr
2 oniatnmai
3 thac wohs
4 aticon
5 ricme radam
6 het wens
7 yelarit ohws
8 mdctnuearyo
9 doprei maard
10 ceydom
11 poas poera
12 cisecen fintioc

2 Choose the genres from Exercise 1.

1
This is a story about a group of men and women in their twenties who hang out together in New York. They see each other all the time and know everything about each other. They keep getting into unusual and embarrassing situations. It's the funniest show I've ever seen – I never stop laughing!

2
This is a film about a superhero and the things he has to do to save the world. The beginning is really exciting, but after that it gets boring. You hear the actors' voices, but you don't see them because they are cartoons.

3
This takes place in a big house with a lot of real people living together who didn't know each other before. They are filmed 24 hours a day. The public watch them while they're doing normal things like eating, talking and sleeping. It's sometimes great fun, but also sometimes sad.

4
I love these kinds of programmes, especially the ones about nature and animals. The images are usually excellent too. I saw one last night about the secret world of spiders!

5
This story takes place in the year 3014 when the world is a very different place. Our hero, a girl aged 16, receives an object from the past from her father. She wants to find out more about it and so she travels back in time. I don't really like this type of film, but it was quite interesting.

6
This takes place in 1900. It's a traditional story about the lives of ordinary men and women at that time. There is a war and life is very hard. The men are fighting and the women are looking after children and the people who are hurt. I love films like this – you see that life was really difficult in the past.

3 Complete the conversations with the words in the boxes.

action	crime	horror

A: Did you see the film last night?
B: Yes, it was great! All those fast car scenes, and you never knew what was going to happen next – a real ¹_____ thriller.
A: Oh, I thought it was a very scary film – you know, a ²_____ film.
B: True! But there was a police officer trying to catch the murderer, so also a ³_____ drama.
A: Yes, it was three films in one!

chat show	the news	soap opera

A: Let's watch that new ⁴_____ everyone is talking about. You know, the one about that group of people living in the same street in London.
B: Oh no, that's boring. I love listening to celebrities talking about their lives. Let's watch the ⁵_____ instead.
A: I don't think listening to celebrities talking about their lives is very interesting. Oh, it's 6 pm – let's watch ⁶_____. We can find out what's happening in the world.
B: OK, but after that we're watching what I want to watch!

documentary	period drama	science fiction

A: What did you think of the film last night?
B: *The Last Jedi*? I loved it! Best ⁷_____ film ever.
A: I know. Did you see the ⁸_____ after it about how they wrote the story?
B: No, Mum wanted to watch that ⁹_____ – so boring, about how members of a rich family got on with each other in the nineteenth century.

READING

So, you want to work in **reality TV**?

1 Tick (✓) the sentences you think are true.

1 Reality shows are great fun to watch. ☐
2 Reality shows are the opposite of real. ☐
3 Reality shows can help you to learn about people. ☐
4 Reality shows have a negative influence on society. ☐

2 Read the article. Answer these questions.

1 Which of the following happens because you work long hours?
  a You are always waiting to be told what to do next.
  b You don't have a very good social life.
  c Your working day is not organised.
2 Why do you have to accept that you won't earn much at first?
  a because other people will be happy to do the job for little money
  b because you will soon start to earn a lot more
  c because you need to get experience doing the job
3 Why is a career in reality TV difficult for some people?
  a because they dislike the people in the show
  b because they don't want people on the show to be happy
  c because they don't like seeing people who are upset
4 What type of person do you have to be to work in reality TV?
  a unfriendly
  b relaxed
  c confident
5 What do you have to do to have a successful career in reality TV?
  a accept the true facts of a situation
  b work well as part of a team
  c have lots of experience in television

3 Match the highlighted words in the text to their meanings.

1 natural skill or ability ....
2 to do something successfully ....
3 a group of people who work together ....
4 time to enjoy with your friends ....
5 prepared and happy to do something ....

4 Complete the sentences with the correct form of the words from Exercise 3.

1 I hang out with my friends every day. My .... is great!
2 I am always .... to help you as much as I can.
3 The production .... on this new film are great fun to work with!
4 That actor has so much .... He is amazing!
5 He stayed calm and relaxed, and .... the situation very well.

If your dream is to work in reality television as part of the crew, then there are some things you need to know before you set out on a career in that direction.

The Hours

Say goodbye to a social life! The working hours in reality TV are often extremely long. You might find yourself working 12- to 18-hour days (sometimes longer). Also, your working day changes all the time, you never know what could happen or when. You are always waiting for someone to tell you what to do next. So when you're working on a reality TV show, you probably won't get together with friends very often.

The Money

Until you have shown the producers that you have talent, salaries are often extremely low. But if you're not willing to work for low pay, there are hundreds of people behind you who will. So, you have to be realistic about what to expect when you're starting out. One day, you might earn a lot of money, but in the beginning, you can expect your bank account to be almost empty.

The Subject Matter

Some people are not able to work in reality TV because they feel sorry for the people on the show. As a crew member of a reality show, you might have to watch people in difficult situations. Although it's human nature to want to help these people, it's also your job to help film these moments for a national or global audience. So you have to be certain about your ability to deal with problems well.

The Reputation

Unfortunately, reality TV has a bad reputation. It's not always a pleasant occupation. And because your job is to film people who are sometimes sad or angry, people might think you are an anti-social person. You will have to manage this on your own. If you can do this, then your reality TV career might be a great success.

1 Choose the two answers that are possible in each sentence.

1 Yesterday I saw a man _____ works at the library.
   a who   b which   c that
2 Tonight we can watch the film _____ stars your favourite actor.
   a who   b that   c which
3 Have you visited the museum _____ is in Lark Street?
   a where   b which   c that
4 The person _____ wrote this story has an amazing imagination.
   a who   b which   c that
5 I find it difficult to read books _____ include long descriptions of places.
   a which   b that   c where
6 My mobile phone is the object _____ I love most!
   a that   b who   c which

2 Choose the correct word.

1 This is a wonderful book *who / that* I'm reading.
2 We went on a tour of the studios in Hollywood *which / where* many famous films were made.
3 Kristen Stewart, *who / which* was in *Snow White and the Huntsman*, is my favourite actress.
4 There's a great site *where / that* you can catch up on TV shows.
5 This is the TV show *which / who* I was telling you about.
6 At my school, there are some people *which / who* can be really annoying.

3 Complete the text with the correct relative pronouns.

4 Complete the sentences with an ending from the box and the correct relative pronoun.

> … takes place on a beach.
> … was in a film about dancing.
> … have Daniel Craig in them.
> … Carole was reading.
> … my mum and dad first met.
> … is showing at the City Theatre.

1 I enjoy all films _____
2 That is the cinema _____
3 This is a great film _____
4 I love that actress _____
5 This is the book _____
6 Ariana wants to see the play _____

5 Choose the correct sentence in each pair.

◉ 1 a There is a space which is very clean and suitable for a picnic.
    b There is a space where is very clean and suitable for a picnic.
2 a Well, I have a friend that is called Manuel.
    b Well, I have a friend that called Manuel.
3 a The only boy let me play with him was Fidel.
    b The only boy who let me play with him was Fidel.
4 a I've chosen the park is near your house because it's a quiet place.
    b I've chosen the park which is near your house because it's a quiet place.
5 a I got a new computer game that is called *Sims 4*.
    b I got a new computer game is called *Sims 4*.

The Hunger Games is an exciting story ¹ _____ takes place in another world. It is about a dangerous competition. The story is about a girl called Katniss and her family and friends. In the story, everyone must watch a terrible competition ² _____ is shown on TV, ³ _____ everyone can see what is happening. When Primrose, ⁴ _____ is Katniss's sister, is chosen, Katniss decides to take her place. In the end, the rules of the competition change. The book and the film starring Jennifer Lawrence are both popular with teens. Many teens ⁵ _____ read the book first wanted to see how different the film was. Some liked the parts ⁶ _____ the characters had to make difficult choices.

Talking about films and shows

1 Add the missing vowels (a, e, i, o, u) to these film-making words.

1 s _ _ _ n d t r _ _ c k
2 p l _ t
3 c h _ _ r _ _ c t _ _ r
4 r _ v _ _ _ w
5 t r _ _ _ l _ _ r
6 c l _ _ p
7 s _ _ r _ _ _ s

2 Match the words from Exercise 1 with their meanings.

1 a number of related events in TV shows
2 a short part of a film
3 a short introduction to a film before it is released
4 the main events in a film's story
5 the music created for a film
6 a person in a film or TV show
7 a piece of writing giving an opinion about a film or TV programme

1 Read the questions and possible answers. Underline the key words.

2 Listen to six conversations. For each question, choose the correct answer.

1 You will hear a girl talking to a friend about a film they've seen.
How does she feel about it?
A confused by parts of the story
B impressed by the quality of the acting
C surprised by the way music was used in it

2 You will hear a boy talking to a friend about going to a cinema.
What was he unhappy about?
A the attitude of the staff
B the range of films shown
C the behaviour of other customers

3 You will hear a boy talking to a friend.
The boy thinks he would like to be a film actor because of
A the people he would meet.
B the money he would earn.
C the attention he would receive.

4 You will hear a girl talking to her friend Peter.
What is she doing?
A complaining about something he's done
B reminding him about a promise he made
C trying to persuade him to change his mind

5 You will hear two friends talking about a television talent show.
What do they agree about?
A The judges are often too rude.
B The audience is mainly younger people.
C The performers are very brave to appear on it.

6 You will hear two friends talking about watching television.
Why has the boy decided to watch television less?
A He wants to spend more time on other things.
B He thinks many programmes are boring.
C He is keen to please his parents.

3 Listen again and check your answers.

TAKE
3

Int Ext Mos
Sync

DIRECTOR

15 DIGITAL LIFE

VOCABULARY Computer phrases

1 Find and circle the computing phrases.

deletehotpasswordshareneverfilepodcastcardoasearchappuploadlemoninstalldownloadsunviruslink

2 Choose the correct word.

1 Oh, no! I've just *installed / deleted* all my work.
2 You should change your *password / podcast* regularly.
3 Have you listened to Jamie's music *podcast / app*?
4 Don't open that email! There's a *link / virus* in it – it'll destroy everything.
5 My sister is doing a *search / password* for information about the planets for her homework.
6 When you've finished your video, *install / upload* it to the website.
7 I've just bought *a file / an app* that tells me when to go to bed!
8 Mia spends a lot of time *sharing / downloading* her photos on Instagram.

3 Complete the crossword using the clues below.

1 This might tell you how many hours you've studied!
2 You can listen to it on your phone or the internet at any time.
3 This is a program that is secretly put on your computer and can damage it.
4 This can be a document or a short video clip.
5 This is usually made up of letters and numbers, and you have to remember it!
6 remove something from a computer's memory
7 If you click on this, it takes you to a website.
8 put a computer program onto a computer so that the computer can use it

4 Complete the text with the correct form of the words from Exercise 1.

Our school has a website that is only for its students. If you have to
¹s_____ a ²f_____, you can do it on the website.
Each student creates their own ³p_____ and then they can
go to the website. Each teacher has ⁴u_____ a lot of useful
⁵l_____ for their subject. There's also an ⁶a_____ for
your phone, which you can ⁷d_____ from the website. It's really
simple to ⁸i_____.

READING

1 Quickly read about the best travel websites and apps. Which three apps let you see what people think about the service?

1 ....

2 ....

3 ....

2 Read the descriptions of the apps. Decide which app would be the most suitable for each teenager.

1 Angela doesn't like driving when she goes on holiday. She likes to know that she can rely on a good service to collect her from the airport and take her to her hotel. She doesn't want to waste time queueing or waiting to be picked up.

2 Steve loves food and eats out as often as he can when he visits a city. He wants to know the best places to eat and how much they will cost. He also wants to be able to make a reservation.

3 Remy likes knowing which places people he knows are visiting when they travel. He also loves knowing the best places to visit at each destination – especially new cafés and restaurants. He also wants to be able to tell other people which places he thinks they should visit.

4 Sacha likes to visit unusual places when he goes on holiday. Before he goes away, he wants to know exactly what he needs to pack. He doesn't like to have to pay to download apps.

5 Becky is a very sociable person and enjoys talking to the local people in the countries she visits. She wants to know how to order food and ask how to get to different places. She doesn't mind paying for apps.

3 Match the highlighted words in the text to their meanings.

1 direction to a destination ....

2 something that says what will happen in the future ....

3 people who have guests ....

4 is much better than other similar things or people ....

Best Travel Apps

Home + Away

Home + Away is an app that allows people to rent places to stay: individual rooms and whole homes in 190 countries. It matches guests with hosts, confirms travel dates and organises payment. In addition, it gives you the opportunity to read guests' reviews about their experience. It's great for people who want a more personal alternative to hotels.

TravelZoom

TravelZoom stands out because of its cool design and social feel. You can read and write reviews of hotels and restaurants you've visited. You can also check on your friends' experiences, find recommendations for places you plan to visit and give advice on any travel topic, such as the best burger in San Francisco!

Jump the Queue

If you don't like queueing for a restaurant while on holiday, this is your website. With more than 40,000 restaurants to choose from, it's the biggest and best app of its kind. It lets you search for places to eat by district, cuisine and customer ratings before booking your table for free, meaning there's no need to wait for a table to become available.

Journey Happy

Do you want to find out how to travel in comfort as well as style? Journey Happy will help you choose a flight based on whether there's good leg room, bigger seats, new planes, faster wi-fi, friendlier cabin crew, fewer passengers and a lot more.

4caster

This free app is perfect for travellers who like to check what the weather will be like. It lets you see what the weather conditions are like in destinations that aren't very well known, like tiny Greek islands or villages in northern Thailand. The forecast gives you the weather in the next hour or for the entire month ahead – so it's good for planning what clothes you need to take with you.

Travelator

If you're going to a country that speaks one of the languages on Travelator, you can learn some useful phrases on this fun language-learning app. The only downside is the price – at $10, it's the most expensive app in our list.

Go-Go City

Go-Go City connects you with professional taxi drivers in 170 cities around the world directly from your smartphone. You can pay by card or cash, and there's no need to queue or wait for a taxi to pass by because the taxi comes to you in under 15 minutes, wherever you are.

City Router

This new app is a free route planner that covers cities in Europe and North America. It's perfect for checking driving times and distances, and it includes other useful tools like weather forecasts and maps that you can download to your phone.

DIGITAL LIFE 61

GRAMMAR — Present simple passive

1 Complete the sentences with the correct form of the present simple passive.

1 The phone _____, so the child has to call an adult. (lock)
2 Many apps _____ with new phones. (give away)
3 Computer games _____ by programmers. (write)
4 English _____ in many countries. (speak)
5 In tourist places, many photos _____. (take)
6 Not much _____ about the latest computer virus. (know)
7 Students _____ to upload their completed projects to the school website. (ask)

2 Rewrite these sentences using the present simple passive.

1 They offer several types of fruit juice on the menu.
_____
2 They use real fruit.
_____
3 They make the drinks in the kitchen behind the café.
_____
4 They bring the drinks to your table.
_____
5 The waiters wear uniforms.
_____
6 They close the café on Sundays.
_____

3 Complete the text with the present simple passive form of the words in the box, as in the example. There is one negative.

| create | delete | design | ~~enjoy~~ | intend |
| see | share | store | use | watch |

Many social media sites [1] _are enjoyed_ by teens and [2] _____ i_____ to give you a different experience. Snapchat [3] _____ d_____ to let you share fun videos and photos just for a moment because, after a short time, the picture disappears. But Snapchat pictures and videos [4] _____ d_____ because the data [5] _____ s_____ somewhere on the internet and so it might last forever.

Photos and text [6] _____ s_____ on Tumblr. When you sign up, a password [7] _____ c_____. These sites [8] _____ u_____ for personal photos and information.

Short videos [9] _____ w_____ on Twitter. Some are funny, but others aren't! If you don't change the settings, everything [10] _____ s_____ by everyone.

4 Correct the mistakes in these sentences, or tick (✓) any you think are correct.

1 My best friend is call Sean.
_____
2 You are invite to the picnic next Saturday.
_____
3 It will be hold in Tao Dan Park.
_____
4 The game can be played by two players.
_____
5 She called Michelle.
_____

VOCABULARY — Phrasal verbs: technology

1 Match the phrasal verbs to their meanings.

1 look up _____
2 plug in _____
3 switch on / turn on _____
4 turn up _____
5 take out _____
6 shut down _____
7 switch off / turn off _____
8 turn down _____

a reduce the level of sound or heat that something produces
b remove something from somewhere
c stop the power on electrical equipment
d find a piece of information in a book or on a computer
e increase the level of sound or heat that a machine produces
f make an electric light, TV, etc. start working
g connect a piece of electrical equipment
h stop an electric light, TV, etc. working

2 Complete the sentences with the words in the box.

| down | off | off |
| on | out | up |

1 Before she goes to bed, Mum turns _____ the TV.
2 It's easy to look _____ information on the computer.
3 It was too hot and so I turned the heating _____ a bit.
4 When you're in the theatre, you have to switch _____ your phone.
5 Have you switched _____ the computer yet? I need it now.
6 Dad and Nathan took the battery _____ of the car.

WRITING An informal email (3)

1 Read part of an email that Akim has received from his friend Sophie. What information does Sophie want from Akim?

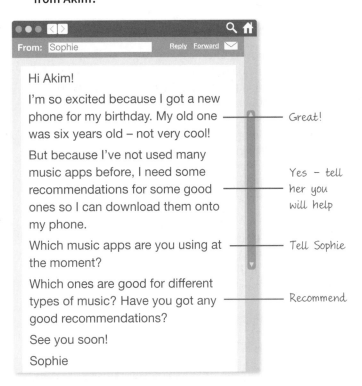

From: Sophie   Reply Forward

Hi Akim!

I'm so excited because I got a new phone for my birthday. My old one was six years old – not very cool! — *Great!*

But because I've not used many music apps before, I need some recommendations for some good ones so I can download them onto my phone. — *Yes – tell her you will help*

Which music apps are you using at the moment? — *Tell Sophie*

Which ones are good for different types of music? Have you got any good recommendations? — *Recommend*

See you soon!

Sophie

2 Read Akim's reply. Does he answer all of Sophie's questions?

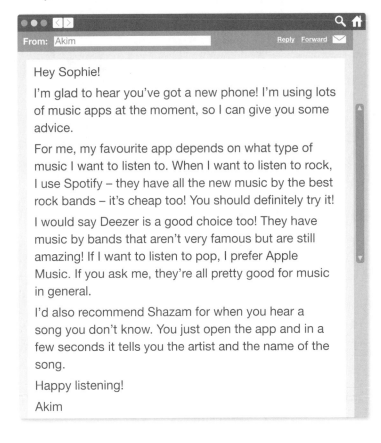

From: Akim   Reply Forward

Hey Sophie!

I'm glad to hear you've got a new phone! I'm using lots of music apps at the moment, so I can give you some advice.

For me, my favourite app depends on what type of music I want to listen to. When I want to listen to rock, I use Spotify – they have all the new music by the best rock bands – it's cheap too! You should definitely try it!

I would say Deezer is a good choice too! They have music by bands that aren't very famous but are still amazing! If I want to listen to pop, I prefer Apple Music. If you ask me, they're all pretty good for music in general.

I'd also recommend Shazam for when you hear a song you don't know. You just open the app and in a few seconds it tells you the artist and the name of the song.

Happy listening!

Akim

3 What phrases does Akim use to recommend things and give his opinion?

1 ....

2 ....

3 ....

4 ....

5 ....

6 ....

4 Complete the sentences with your opinions about game apps. Compare your opinions with a partner. Do you agree with your partner's opinions?

1 In my opinion, ...

2 I really think ....

3 I would say, ...

5 What informal phrases does Akim use to begin and end his email?

....

6 Read Sophie's email in Exercise 1 again. Plan your reply and make some notes. Here are some ideas to help you.

- How many music apps do you have on your phone?
- How often do you use them?
- What's your favourite music app? Why do you like it?
- Which is the cheapest?
- What music apps would you recommend to your friends?

7 Write your email to Sophie.

- Use the tips in the *Prepare to write* box.
- Write about 100 words.
- Remember to check your spelling and grammar.

VOCABULARY Doing experiments

1 Add the missing vowels (a, e, i, o, u) to complete these words for doing experiments.

1 b l __ w
2 b __ __ l
3 c __ v __ r
4 f __ ll
5 p __ __ r

6 r __ b
7 s h __ k __
8 s t __ r
9 t __ __
10 w r __ p

2 Look at the pictures. What are they doing? Write an experiment word from Exercise 1 in each space.

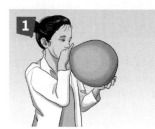

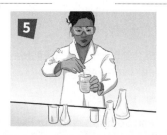

3 Complete the sentences with the correct form of the words from Exercise 1.

1 Water _____ at a temperature of 100 degrees.
2 By _____ the place where you blow into the balloon, the air stays inside in the balloon.
3 To start the experiment, you need to _____ the glass with cardboard.
4 _____ the paper around the bottle and leave it for five minutes.
5 After you have _____ the balloon on your hair, move it away from the can and watch the can move towards the balloon.

4 Match the questions and answers.

1 How is Charlie going to get air inside the balloon? ....
2 How do you get the different liquids to mix well? ....
3 What do you need to do with the water before you cook the egg? ....
4 When you want to mix sugar with coffee, what do you do? ....
5 If the glasses don't have enough water in them, what should I do? ....

a Pour it into a saucepan and boil it.
b Stir it!
c He's going to blow into it.
d Fill them to the top.
e You shake them a lot.

READING

1 Tick the inventions that you think were made by mistake. Read the text quickly to check your answers.

1 the internet
2 a popular soft drink
3 the first antibiotic
4 a popular type of biscuit

2 Read the article and complete the sentences with one or two words in each space.

1 Spencer Silver accidentally made a glue that was easy to take off and didn't _____ the paper or pages it was stuck to.

2 Art Fry found that the glue didn't make the pages of his books dirty and so was very good for _____.

3 Constantine Fahlberg left a chemical on his hands by mistake, and while eating his lunch he found that his bread tasted unusually _____.

4 Saccharine is used instead of _____ to make soft drinks.

5 Alexander Fleming noticed that _____ weren't growing around the mould.

6 He realised that the substance could be used to cure _____.

7 Ruth Wakefield didn't have the right kind of _____.

8 The chocolate and dough didn't _____ together.

3 Match the highlighted words in the text to their meanings.

1 a mixture made of flour and water used to make bread, biscuits and cakes _____

2 a substance used to stick things together _____

3 something that grows on old food _____

4 an artificial substance that has a similar taste to sugar _____

5 a room for doing scientific tests _____

4 Complete the sentences with the correct form of the words from Exercise 3.

1 Don't eat that! It's got _____ on it.

2 Diet cola is the same as normal cola, but it contains a _____ instead of sugar.

3 You have to wear special glasses to protect your eyes when working in the _____.

4 After you've made the _____, put it in the oven.

5 It hasn't stuck properly. This _____ isn't very strong!

Inventions
that changed the world but were made by mistake

When you think of people who have invented something that has changed the world, you immediately think of the achievements of some very intelligent scientists. But their success often comes in an unexpected way. Did you know that the medicine penicillin was discovered because of a mistake? It's amazing to think that something that was an accident then became something that the whole world now uses to stop serious illness.

Here are a few examples of inventions that were made by mistake:

Sticky notes
In 1968, scientist Spencer Silver created a type of glue that would stick to things but could be removed easily from any surface. He was really trying to create a super-strong glue but failed. Art Fry, another scientist, was tired of his bookmarks falling out of his books. He remembered Silver's special glue and wondered if this might be the answer to his problem. When he tried the glue on his bookmarks, they stuck and didn't damage the pages. It worked. It was then that he thought of the idea of using the glue on notes.

Saccharine
Saccharine was discovered in 1879 by the chemist Constantine Fahlberg while he was working in his university laboratory. The discovery came because he forgot to wash his hands after spilling a chemical on them, and when he was eating his bread at lunch it tasted unusually sweet. It was later produced in huge quantities as an artificial sweetener and is now used in soft drinks to reduce the sugar and calories.

Penicillin
Scientist Alexander Fleming invented penicillin, which helps stop infections by killing bacteria. He was on holiday and he had left a petri dish (a special dish used by scientists to grow bacteria) in his laboratory. When he returned, the dish had an unusual mould on it, but there were no bacteria growing. He realised that something in the mould was killing the bacteria. He also realised that if you use this substance on the human body, it stops serious illness. This became the first antibiotic, penicillin, which has saved millions of people's lives over the years.

Chocolate-chip cookies
In the 1930s, Ruth Wakefield owned a very popular restaurant called the Toll House Inn in the United States. While making some chocolate cookies, she discovered she had no special baker's chocolate left and decided to use some normal chocolate instead. She poured it into the dough, but the chocolate did not mix with the dough and this was how the chocolate-chip cookie was born.

As Mark Twain said: 'Name the greatest of all inventors. Accident.' Many great inventions are the result of the creative use of a mistake.

1 Complete the zero conditional sentences using the correct form of the verbs in brackets in the correct order.

1 If you .... your experiment work, you .... happy. (feel, see)
2 If you .... water, it .... at 100 °C. (boil, heat)
3 I .... always exhausted the next day if I .... to bed very late. (be, go)
4 They .... the schools in the United States if the temperature .... to –20 °C. (close, drop)
5 If my brother .... under a ladder, he .... he will have bad luck. (think, walk)
6 My sister .... her science classes if she .... in a group with her friends. (work, enjoy)

2 Complete the text with the correct form of the verbs in the box.

become	get	go
pour	make	say

There is a hole in my roof. When it rains, the water
¹............... in. When the water comes in, it
²............... the floor wet. When the floor is wet, the walls ³............... green. When the walls are green, I ⁴............... ill. When I am ill, I ⁵............... to the doctor. When I see the doctor, he always ⁶............... the same thing: 'Fix the roof!'

3 Match the sentence halves.

1 If you freeze water, ...
2 If you take penicillin, ...
3 If you pour oil on water, ...
4 If you don't water plants, ...
5 If you heat ice, ...

a it becomes liquid.
b they will die.
c it will become solid.
d it will kill the infection.
e it floats.

4 Complete the text with the correct form of the verbs.

My mum enjoys talking about science because she studied it at university. If someone ¹*is / will be* interested, she shares her knowledge with them because she ²*believes / doesn't believe* that one of the main benefits of having knowledge is that you can pass it on to other people. If there ³*is / will be* a science programme on TV, she ⁴*will watch / won't watch* it. Last week she was really disappointed because her favourite science TV show wasn't on. If this happens, she ⁵*reads / will read* her science magazine instead. I'm really lucky that my mum is good at science because if I have science homework, she ⁶*helps / will help* me with it. Last week our teacher gave our test results back and I got a good mark. If I have children one day, I ⁷*share / will share* my knowledge with them too.

5 Choose the correct sentence in each pair.

⊙ 1 a If you'll meet her, I'm sure that you'll like her.
    b If you meet her, I'm sure that you'll like her.
  2 a If you don't go with us, you'll missed out on a lot of fun.
    b If you don't go with us, you'll miss out on a lot of fun.
  3 a If you go, we'll have a better time.
    b If you will go, we'll have a better time.
  4 a It'll be a pleasure if you came.
    b It'll be a pleasure if you come.
  5 a If he doesn't smile, I know he's not happy with me.
    b If he doesn't smile, I know he will be not happy with me.

VOCABULARY

1 Choose the correct preposition from the box to make science phrasal verbs.

away	out	up

1 cut _____ (a sheet of paper)
2 carry _____ (an experiment)
3 work _____ (an answer)
4 blow _____ (a building)
5 take _____ (numbers)
6 add _____ (numbers)

2 Complete the sentences with a phrasal verb from Exercise 1.

1 Be careful! If you mix those two liquids, you will _____ the lab!
2 I need to _____ the best way to design the experiment.
3 If I _____ the two amounts, I can see the total.
4 You have to _____ the liquid from the heat and then leave it to cool for ten minutes.
5 It's best to _____ the experiment yourself and then show the class.
6 I will _____ the bread into small pieces, then feed the ducks.

LISTENING

1 You will hear an interview with a scientist called Anna Millward, who is an expert on fish.

For each question, choose the correct answer. Then listen again and check that the other two options are wrong.

1 Anna first became interested in fish when
   A she read about some in a book.
   B she studied some at school.
   C she saw some in a zoo.
2 Why did Anna give up the idea of becoming a vet?
   A The training course was too long for her.
   B Seeing sick animals made her feel bad.
   C Her interest in animals changed.
3 What is the main aim of Anna's research?
   A to discover new types of fish
   B to find out about where fish live
   C to develop new ways of protecting fish
4 What part of her job does Anna find most difficult?
   A getting used to conditions in different countries
   B spending a lot of time working in a laboratory
   C communicating with a wide range of people
5 Why is Anna keen to talk to fishermen?
   A to persuade them to catch fish that she wants to study
   B to make them aware that some fish are disappearing
   C to use their knowledge of fish for her research
6 Anna says we should
   A only eat fish caught near to where we live.
   B remember the benefits of eating fish.
   C reduce the amount of fish we eat.

17 TALENTED

VOCABULARY — Arts and entertainment

1 Complete the crossword using the clues below.

1 someone who has written something
2 a picture created with paint
3 a room or building which is used for showing works of art
4 a film company or a place where films are made
5 a piece of art that is made from stone, wood, clay, etc.
6 someone who practises one of the arts
7 someone who writes books or the words for a film
8 the life story of a person written by someone else
9 a book that tells a story about imaginary people and events
10 writing that often rhymes
11 someone who performs in films and TV shows
12 the people who sit and watch a performance at a theatre
13 someone who writes poems

2 Choose the odd one out.

0	painting	poetry	sculpture	(audience)
1	novel	script	poet	biography
2	exhibition	gallery	studio	novel
3	filming	director	script	artist
4	poet	painter	writer	sculpture
5	drawings	paintings	sculpture	author
6	director	writer	actor	painter

3 Complete the text with the words in the box. There is one word you don't need.

drawings	exhibition	gallery
painter	paintings	poet
poetry	sculpture	series

Last week I went to an ¹ _____
called 'Chickens'. It was held in the local art
² _____ and it showed the work of a local
³ _____, Katija Vorelli, amongst others. As
we arrived, we saw an enormous ⁴ _____
of a chicken outside the building! Then we
went inside. Katija usually only does colourful
⁵ _____, but this time she included some
pencil ⁶ _____. The ⁷ _____
Ricardo Peters was also there and he read some of
his ⁸ _____. It was a fun evening and gave
me some ideas for my own paintings and drawings.

READING

1 Read the article quickly and choose the best title.

Singer Lorde to make her acting debut
in new film ☐

Lorde – a rising star with a bright future ☐

New Zealand pop star Lorde fails to
achieve success abroad ☐

2 Read the first two paragraphs of the article again and think of the word which best fits each space. Use only one word in each gap.

Every month we feature a different artist. Here is a star from New Zealand who has made a big name for herself.

Bio

Ella Marija Lani Yelich-O'Connor is a singer-songwriter, but she is better known by her stage name, Lorde. The daughter of a well-known poet, Sonja Yelich, she grew (1) _____ in Auckland. (2) _____ the age of 12, she was spotted in a school talent show by someone from a music company, and (3) _____ of this, she was offered a recording contract with Universal Music New Zealand.

Success

She became (4) _____ first female artist in 17 years to get to the top of the song chart, and in 2014 she won two Grammy awards. (5) _____ was for the best song of the year, 'Royals', and the other was for the best individual performance. She (6) _____ continued to win many more prizes since then.

Connecting with fans

Social media is an obvious way to stay in touch with your fans, and Lorde regularly uploads photos to her Instagram account and writes about what she's doing on Twitter. One of her social media followers told her she wanted to do lots of school projects about her. The artist replied, saying she really liked doing school projects and she loved the idea that someone wanted to do one on her. By reading her comments and posts, it's easy to see why people love her. She sings about personal topics that lots of people can relate to.

What's next?

Lorde released her second album, *Melodrama*, in 2017, which went to number one in the album charts of the United States, Canada, Australia and New Zealand. But as she grows older, will she continue singing? Or will she do something completely different, like acting or writing novels?

What do you think?

She's just the best. She's got the talent to do anything she wants. Go, Lorde!
@rainbows

There are so many singers who, after they finish their third album, fade away.
She seems really nice, though, and if she continues to work hard, she will be successful for a long time.
@love34

I don't know. She's got a great voice, but that's all. People will get bored of her and someone else will appear. Musicians these days aren't like the old greats.
@fl ea_pea02

Hide comments

3 **Read the article again. Decide if each sentence is correct (C), incorrect (I), or not mentioned (NM).**

1 The singer uses part of her real name as her stage name.
2 The singer's mother is famous for writing poetry.
3 She was the first female artist to get to number one in the charts.
4 The last awards she won were two Grammy awards.
5 She was upset that a fan wanted to do a project about her.
6 Lorde tries to reply to every social media message she receives from her fans.
7 Her second album hasn't been very successful.
8 Lorde is planning to write her first book next year.

4 **Match the highlighted words in the text to their meanings.**

1 the sounds someone makes when they speak or sing
2 a legal agreement signed by two people or companies
3 lists of the most popular songs or albums each week
4 slowly disappear
5 the name an actor or singer uses instead of their real name

Reported commands

1 Add the missing vowels (a, e, i, o, u) to make reporting verbs.

1 w __ r n
2 __ s k
3 __ r d __ r
4 t __ l l
5 __ d v __ s __
6 p __ r s __ __ d __
7 r __ m __ n d
8 c __ n v __ n c __

2 Write the words in the correct order to make sentences.

1 near / us / warned / not / He / the water / to go

2 explain / We / the artist's ideas / the teacher / asked / to

3 ordered / The / us / be / headteacher / quiet / to

4 me / Billy / my / eyes / to / not / open / told

5 with / advised / again / to / not / me / her / Lorraine / argue

6 persuaded / Felix / to / buy / the latest PlayStation / his parents

7 us / Dad / the school trip / to / give / the details / reminded / about / him

8 me / to / the school film night / Mum / convinced / go / to

3 Complete the comments. Use the reporting verbs in brackets and add any other words you need.

1 'You should go round the art exhibition together,' said the man.
The man _____ round the art exhibition together. (advise)

2 'Show me your tickets, please,' said the security man.
The security man _____ our tickets. (ask)

3 'Wait at the door!' he said.
He _____ at the door. (order)

4 'You mustn't walk there!' said the woman.
The woman _____ there. (warn)

5 'Remove all phones from your bags, please.'
He _____ all our phones from our bags. (tell)

6 'Let's go to the café first!' said Kari.
Kari _____ to the café first. (persuade)

7 Don't forget to take your guitar to school for your music lesson.
My dad _____ to school. (remind)

8 'Don't go and see the new exhibition at the gallery – it's terrible.'
She _____ the new exhibition at the gallery. (convince)

4 Complete the report of the conversation with the correct form of the reporting verbs in box A and the verbs in box B.

A | ask | persuade | remind | tell

B | add | go | help | not get

Dad: Lili, can you help me with the dinner?
Lili: Sure. Remember, Josh is coming for dinner, so add some extra meat for him!
Dad: Yeah, sure. Do you think you could go to the shops to get some more for me?
Lili: Oh, Dad, really?
Dad: Well, I also want to make a pudding and there isn't any chocolate.
Lili: I'm going now!
Dad: Don't get milk chocolate, please – I need dark.

Dad ¹ _____ Lili ² _____ him with dinner. Lili ³ _____ Dad ⁴ _____ more meat for Josh. Dad ⁵ _____ Lili ⁶ _____ to the shops for him. Dad ⁷ _____ Lili ⁸ _____ milk chocolate because he needed dark chocolate.

5 Correct the mistakes in these sentences or tick (✓) any you think are correct.

1 She said to me to look out of the window to check the weather.

2 She told me give back the money.

3 We were in the same class and the teacher asked for us to do a project together.

4 We were both playing football at the club, and the trainer told us to play together.

5 We were talking and a boy in front of us tell us be quiet.

1 Make adjectives from these nouns. Use -al or -ful.

1 help
2 nature
3 environment
4 profession
5 peace
6 stress
7 pain
8 culture
9 politics
10 music
11 success
12 tradition
13 colour

2 Complete the documentary review with the correct form of the words in brackets.

I watched this [1] _____ (origin) documentary on the TV last night. It was interesting and full of [2] _____ (culture) information. It described the [3] _____ (finance) situation of the biggest [4] _____ (nation) music festival in the UK. It wasn't a very [5] _____ (cheer) report because the organisers have almost run out of money. However, they're [6] _____ (hope) that they won't have to cancel the festival. But it was [7] _____ (use) to know more about it. A lot of the documentary took place in [8] _____ (centre) Liverpool, where the festival headquarters are. I'm not sure what the answers to the problem are, but it was a [9] _____ (wonder) documentary, which gives the audience a much clearer idea of the topic.

WRITING — A biography

>> See *Prepare to write* box, Student's Book, page 101.

1 Look at the photo. Who is she? What do know about her? Read the biography and check your ideas.

Emma Stone is an American actress. She was born in 1988 in Scottsdale, Arizona. Stone began acting at the age of four and her first performance was in a theatre production of *The Wind in the Willows* in 2000. As a teenager, she moved to Los Angeles with her mother and got a part in her first television show, *In Search of the New Partridge Family* (2004), but it never appeared on TV. By the time she was 19, she was already a winner of a Young Hollywood Award for her film debut in *Superbad*, and she received positive media attention for a part she played in the film *Zombieland*. This led to her getting her first starring role in the teen comedy *Easy A*, which earned her nominations for a Golden Globe Award for Best Actress. This was followed by further success in *The Amazing Spiderman* and the romantic comedy *Crazy, Stupid, Love*. After the success of the Oscar-winning musical *La La Land* in 2017, Stone became the highest-paid actress in the world. When she's not acting, she supports various charities, such as the Cancer Research Institute and the Worldwide Orphans Institute.

2 Read the biography again. What interesting facts do you learn about Emma Stone?

3 How many important dates are mentioned in the biography? What happened in each year?

4 Complete the sentences about people's life stages with one word in each space.

1 He left home _____ the age of 14.
2 She got married _____ she was 21.
3 He started playing football _____ a young child.
4 _____, she's a well-known guitarist.
5 _____ the _____ he started at college, he was already in two bands.

5 You are going to write a biography. Choose a famous person or someone you know. Plan your biography and make some notes. Here are some ideas to help you.

- When were they born?
- What are the important dates in their life?
- What are their main achievements?
- What interesting facts do you know about them?

6 Write your biography.

- Use your notes to help you.
- Remember to check your spelling and grammar.
- Write about 150 words.

18 THE WORLD OF WORK

VOCABULARY | Jobs

1 Complete the puzzle using the clues below, then find the hidden word. Which person

1 teaches people to improve at a sport?
2 makes decisions for a political organisation?
3 designs houses and buildings?
4 gives you legal advice?
5 builds houses and properties?
6 looks after young children?
7 gives medical care to animals that are ill or hurt?
8 writes for newspapers or magazines?
9 prepares or sells medicines?
10 appears on television or radio?
11 stops fires from burning?

Hidden word: ....

2 Read what these teens want to do. Choose a suitable job for them.

1 ....

I want to work with people and I'd like to help them. I like working in a team and I don't mind being in dangerous situations.

2 ....

I want to do a job where I can write. I love writing and giving opinions. But I don't want to be sitting at a desk all day. I want to be with people and ask them questions.

3 ....

I want to create things. I'd really like to draw pictures of buildings that people can live in, or hotels or museums. I think that would be awesome.

4 ....

I love being in front of a camera and communicating information to lots of people. I'm really passionate about doing interviews with interesting people.

5 ....

I don't really know what I want to do. But I think while I'm at university, I'll get a part-time job working with little children. I think that would be good.

6 ....

My friend wants to help people with legal problems. She loves it when people get what they deserve – good or bad.

7 ....

I like being outside. I'm quite strong and I don't mind lifting heavy weights. I'd like to do a job where I'm helping to make something useful and perhaps beautiful.

3 Choose the odd one out.

0 You might work with children in this job.
babysitter coach presenter (builder)
1 You read and write a lot in these jobs.
journalist politician lawyer coach
2 You must be fit to do these jobs.
coach firefighter builder lawyer
3 You might appear on TV in these jobs.
politician journalist model vet

4 You often work in an office in these jobs.
lawyer architect politician model
5 You work with computers in this job.
architect journalist lawyer babysitter
6 You have to study at university to do this job.
lawyer vet architect politician

1 Think about three jobs you would love to do. Write them below.

1 _____ 2 _____ 3 _____

2 Read the article about finding your dream job and add the correct headings (a–f) to the paragraphs (1–5). There is one heading you don't need.

a Put your heart into your work
b Working well with people
c Think about your skills and interests
d Informal interviewing
e Think about what motivates you
f How do you find your dream job?

3 Read the article again. Choose the correct answer.

1 The text says that finding a job that satisfies you _____
  A can make your working life really happy.
  B can have a positive effect on all of your life.

2 The author says that you need to look at yourself realistically _____
  A when you go looking for a job.
  B before you decide what to do.

3 To find out more information, it's a good idea to have interviews that are _____
  A traditional.
  B casual.

4 When you have found a place where you would like to work, you should _____
  A do the job to the best of your ability.
  B do everything right.

5 When you work hard and to a high standard, you _____
  A don't have the time or energy to search for other jobs.
  B discover whether the job is right for you or not.

6 The best thing you can do is _____
  A find a job that pays you well and that you enjoy.
  B find a job that you like and are happy to do.

7 The author's advice is to _____
  A find a job that you're naturally good at and can do extremely well.
  B find a job where you can use your abilities so the work isn't too hard.

4 Match the highlighted words in the text to their meanings.

1 when two options are possible but the result is the same _____
2 how good someone is at doing something compared with other people _____
3 choose from a number or group _____
4 choices you make after thinking about something _____
5 something difficult that requires effort _____

5 Complete the sentences with the correct form of the highlighted words from the text.

1 I'm not sure if she likes or dislikes me. _____, I don't care.
2 I've got to make a _____ about the type of job I want.
3 Being a manager isn't easy. It's a big _____ .
4 The _____ of English spoken in this company is high. Most people are bilingual.
5 Congratulations! You have been _____ for the director's job.

Finding your dream job

1 _____
Finding the perfect job is a big challenge. Getting a job that satisfies you and keeping it can make a big difference to happiness in your whole life. How do you do this?
Here are four tips to help you find your dream job.

2 _____
First, before making any decisions, you need to look at yourself honestly and think about what you love to do and what you are good at. After that, it's time to ask yourself a key question: 'What do I really enjoy doing and what kind of a job can I do that will allow me to do what I enjoy doing?'

3 _____
Instead of having a traditional formal interview, it's better to try to organise informal meetings with possible employers and people in the industry you've identified as a good fit for you and your skills. Find out as much as you can from them about the business, their specific companies, the position you would like and other details about the industry.

4 _____
Once you have found a job, it is very important to give your energy and time to doing your job really, really well. When you do this, one of two things will happen – you might find that this is the right career for you, or you might find that it is not the right career for you and that you need to continue searching. Either way, by working hard and doing the best job you can, you will find the answer much quicker.

5 _____
The best thing you can do for yourself is to select the kind of work that you love and enjoy. You need to find a job where you can use your natural talents and abilities at a high level. You must find a job that inspires you to want to become excellent at what you're doing. Do these things, and you will have a better chance of finding happiness and job satisfaction.

1 Match the sentence halves.

1 I'd buy a new mobile phone ....
2 If you could visit South America, ...
3 How would you feel if ....
4 If you didn't talk so much, ...
5 If you apologised, ...
6 If you looked more carefully, ...
7 Would you feel better ....

a you would hear everything the teacher said.
b I would forgive you.
c if you sat down?
d which country would you choose?
e you would find your pen.
f you lost your new sunglasses?
g if I had enough money.

2 Complete the second conditional sentences with the correct form of the verbs in brackets.

1 I .... the bus here, if I .... you. (not catch, be)
2 If you .... more exercise, you .... better. (do, feel)
3 I .... her to my account if I .... her Instagram name. (add, know)
4 If she .... an umbrella, she .... wet. (have, not get)
5 Bob .... his family on holiday if he .... the lottery. (take, win)
6 I .... on the school trip if I .... so ill. (go, not feel)
7 If I .... a famous person, I .... them lots of questions! (meet, ask)
8 .... to the music festival if I .... you a ticket? (go, give)

3 Complete the text with the correct form of the verbs in the box.

become	become	get	go	happen
look	practise	see	study	study

People often ask what I want to do in the future. If I ¹ .... into the future, what ² ....? If I ³ .... harder, I ⁴ .... better marks. If that ⁵ ...., I ⁶ .... university to study law. If I ⁷ .... law, I ⁸ .... a lawyer. But I don't want to! I want to be a musician! I love playing the guitar, but if I ⁹ .... every day, ¹⁰ .... a famous musician? I wish I could see into the future!

4 Rewrite the sentences using the second conditional.

1 It's raining, so we can't go to the beach.
   If it ...., we ....
2 I haven't got a bike and so I can't cycle to your house.
   If I ...., I ....
3 I can't buy that video game because I haven't got any money.
   If I ...., I ....
4 The film is on too late, so I'm not going to watch it.
   If the film ....,
   I ....
5 We don't buy that ice cream because it is expensive.
   If that ice cream ...., we
   ....

5 Choose the correct sentence in each pair.

1 a Mum promised the children she would buy some sweets for them.
   b Mum promised the children she will bought some sweets for them.
2 a She would leave what she was doing if I needed her to.
   b She would leave what she was doing if I need her to.
3 a My parents would be very happy if you accept.
   b My parents would be very happy if you accepted.
4 a I think if you met him, you would like him.
   b I think if you met him, you will like him.
5 a Then I remembered that if I don't find it, they would not let me take the class.
   b Then I remembered that if I didn't find it, they would not let me take the class.

VOCABULARY — Suffixes: -er, -or, -ist, -ian

1 Complete the words with the correct suffix.

1 film direct
2 guitar
3 music
4 blog
5 reception
6 run
7 support
8 act
9 bake
10 goalkeep
11 novel
12 comedy

2 What do you call someone who

1 manages a school?
2 writes music?
3 visits a place?
4 doesn't eat meat?
5 cleans?
6 creates art for a job?
7 fixes electrical equipment?

3 Write the letters in the correct order to make jobs.

1 akenbr
2 verdir
3 botofaerll
4 toruah
5 petiortmoc
6 tendsti
7 iapints
8 tecsitnis

LISTENING

1 Match the words to the meanings.

1 deadline
2 schedule
3 manage

a organise or control something
b a list of dates and times that shows when things will happen
c a time by which something must be done

🔊 12 2 Listen to the conversations. Answer the questions.

1 What are Sebastian and Nicola's problems?
2 Who are they asking for advice?
3 Do you agree with the advice?

🔊 12 3 Listen again. Are the sentences true (T) or false (F)?

Conversation 1
1 Sebastian has to finish some work by a specific time.
2 Sarah suggests that Sebastian talks to his boss.
3 Sebastian doesn't have a good relationship with his boss.
4 Sarah thinks Sebastian's boss won't understand his situation.

Conversation 2
5 Nicola is not very good at planning her working day.
6 Nicola writes reminders on bits of paper to try to improve things.
7 Amy thinks Nicola is successful in managing her time.
8 Amy says she can help Nicola a few days a week.

🔊 12 4 Listen again. How did the people say the following?

1 I have a lot of work that I haven't completed yet.

2 give you more time to complete the work

3 happy to give you support

4 I'm not getting any better.

5 pay attention to something at the latest time possible

6 My week is filled with a lot of work.

VOCABULARY Things that you read

1 Find 10 words for things that you read in the word square (→ ↓ ↘).

R	B	J	M	B	Y	M	D	G	S	S	I
K	P	E	-	B	O	O	K	R	Y	S	C
S	T	A	B	J	D	Q	K	A	B	T	F
E	D	U	P	B	R	P	N	P	K	I	C
S	N	Z	E	E	D	B	O	H	K	C	S
P	O	S	T	E	R	R	C	I	T	K	A
G	T	A	A	N	B	O	G	C	Z	E	R
K	E	R	D	O	D	C	A	N	U	R	T
Q	Q	Q	U	V	S	H	C	O	U	F	I
A	X	Z	I	E	E	U	C	V	B	K	C
F	D	W	S	L	A	R	T	E	C	L	L
O	N	O	T	I	C	E	T	L	S	T	E

2 Match the words from Exercise 1 to their meanings.

1 a small magazine containing pictures and information on a product or company
2 gives you important information about something
3 an electronic version of a book
4 something you write on with a pen
5 a large printed picture or notice that you put on a wall
6 information placed in a magazine, on TV or on social media that's designed to sell a product or service
7 a story told with pictures
8 a piece of writing on a specific subject in a newspaper or magazine
9 a small piece of paper that's easy to remove from a surface
10 a short message

3 Complete the sentences with the correct word from Exercise 1.

1 You can download the new Harry Potter .... on your computer.
2 Dad left you a ...., telling you that dinner is in the fridge.
3 Quick, get some .... I need to write down this idea!
4 Have you seen that new .... selling dog food? It's so funny!
5 Let's have a look at the holiday .... to see the prices for Greece.
6 I read a really interesting .... about robots in my monthly magazine.
7 I've just bought this great .... for my bedroom wall.
8 Have you seen the .... about the gym class being cancelled?
9 I want to buy that new .... – it's got amazing drawings!
10 To show that you've paid for parking, you have to put a .... inside the car window.

1 List different reasons for notes, notices and adverts.

1 ....
2 ....
3 ....
4 ....

2 Look at the text in each question. What does it say? Choose the correct letter, A, B or C.

1

Stephanie,

If you want to apply for your driving licence, you need to complete the application form. Can you do this by Friday this week, so I can send it?

Mum

Stephanie's mum is telling Stephanie to
A do something by a specific time.
B send her application form herself.
C show her the application form.

2
COMPETITION
Win a smartphone!
Answer the question on the back of the cereal box. People of all ages can enter.

A Only people who eat the cereal can enter.
B You have to be an adult to enter.
C Anyone can enter the competition.

3 **SECURITY NOTICE**
Please wait at the gate for a member of staff. You must display your student ID to staff before entering the library.

A You can only enter the library with a member of staff.
B You can enter the library once you have shown your identification.
C You must collect new ID cards from staff.

4

Rachel,

I've got an exam tomorrow at 10 am and my alarm clock isn't working, so could you wake me up at 8? I don't want to be late for the exam!

Tim

A Tim wants Rachel to take him to his exam.
B Tim is reminding Rachel they have an exam in the morning.
C Tim would like Rachel to do him a favour.

5 **CAUTION!**
There are dangerous chemicals in the science lab. You must wear protective clothing at all times. If you don't know what you should wear, speak to Mr Clarke.

A You have to ask Mr Clarke for permission to enter the science lab.
B It's always necessary to wear special clothes in the science lab.
C Mr Clarke will tell you when you need to wear protective clothing in the science lab.

3 Match the highlighted words in the texts with their meanings.

1 show ....
2 a formal written request for something ....
3 something that you use to wake up in the morning ....
4 giving protection ....
5 take part in ....

4 Complete the sentences with the highlighted words from the text.

1 I'm going to .... the next London Marathon.
2 You're late getting up! Didn't you hear your .... earlier?
3 Please .... your passport at the check-in desk.
4 Sunscreen is a .... cream that you put on your skin to help stop it being damaged by the sun.
5 My .... has been accepted. I'm going to university next year!

GRAMMAR Reported speech

1 Match the direct speech (1–4) to the reported speech (a–d).

1 'I write for the blog,' she said. ....
2 'I'm writing for the blog,' she said. ....
3 'I'll write for the blog,' she said. ....
4 'I can write for the blog,' she said. ....

a She said she could write for the blog.
b She said she was writing for the blog.
c She said she wrote for the blog.
d She said she would write for the blog.

2 Rewrite these sentences using reported speech.

1 'She's reading an interesting article.'
   Emma said ....
2 'Mrs Jones will help me next week.'
   Ben said ....
3 'I don't want to buy a new computer.'
   Fatima said ....
4 'I love downloading free e-books.'
   My brother said ....
5 'Dad can't get here on time.'
   Mum said ....
6 'I'll get some holiday brochures for Japan.'
   My mum said ....
7 'Jo's dad can pick us up.'
   Alison said ....
8 'We won't be there.'
   They said ....

3 Read these video profiles and then report what the people said.

> Hi! I'm Cassie. I'm 15 and I live in the USA. I'm studying for exams now. Then in the summer, I'll go to Camp Kanosia. I love it there because I can swim and do lots of water sports.

1 Cassie said ....
....
....
....

> Hi! I'm Paolo. I'm 14 and I'm from South Africa. I'm making this video profile at the moment! Next year, I'll go to a different school. It's an art school and I can study drawings, paintings and sculpture there.

2 Paolo said ....
....
....
....

4 Correct the mistakes in these sentences or tick (✓) any you think are correct.

1 Jane called me, and she said that she and her brother are going to buy some graphic novels.
....

2 He said that he is going to put the notice in the students' room.
....

3 I want to say you that I got a new e-book.
....

4 She saw me and she say that she knew me, and we began to talk.
....

5 They said that they would get some paper for the printer.
....

VOCABULARY say, speak, talk and tell

1 Complete the conversation with the correct form of *say*, *speak*, *talk* or *tell*. Use some words more than once.

Paul: Hello, is that Cara?
Cara: Yes. Who's ¹ .... ?
Paul: It's Paul. I'm calling to invite you to my party on Saturday.
Cara: I'm sorry. Can you ² .... that again? I can't hear you very well.
Paul: I ³ ...., would you like to come to my party on Saturday?
Cara: Yes, I'd love to! My cousin's here on holiday. Can she come too?
Paul: Yes, of course. ⁴ .... her she's welcome.
Cara: OK, thanks, I'll ⁵ .... her. I've got to go now. It was nice ⁶ .... to you. See you on Saturday!

2 Choose the correct word to complete the sentences.

1 Can you .... me what you mean?
   a speak   b tell   c say
2 Mum can .... four languages.
   a say   b talk   c speak
3 What did you .... ? I couldn't hear you.
   a speak   b talk   c say
4 It's always nice to .... to my best friend.
   a talk   b tell   c say

» See *Prepare to write* box, Student's Book, page 111.

1 Which websites do you visit to read books or reviews? What is a book review? How are they helpful when you want to read a new book?

2 Read the review quickly. Tick (✓) the information that Sam includes.

1 the title of the book ☐
2 the author's name ☐
3 information about the author ☐
4 the name of the main characters ☐
5 the story of the whole book ☐
6 a description of part of the story ☐
7 details about how the story ends ☐
8 his own opinion of the book ☐

REVIEW ★★★★

Divergent
by Veronica Roth

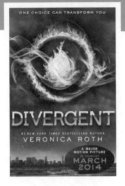

In the Chicago of the distant future, 16-year-old Tris Prior chooses to live in the 'brave' section of the city, where members compete physically with each other to prove their strength. During the initiation process, which is very violent and kills or seriously injures a few characters, Tris becomes attracted to her handsome instructor, Four, so it's also quite romantic! But violence increases towards the end of the book, resulting in many lives being lost. I loved Tris Prior. Like *The Hunger Games* heroine, Katniss Everdeen, she is a strong, generous female character. It's a wonderful, exciting story, but that's all I'm going to tell you! Read it!

Reviewed by Sam R, Manchester

3 Read the information below and find the four features in Sam's review.

In an online book review:
- include the title of the book and the author.
- include the name of the main character.
- include some details of the story, but not all.
- give your opinion of the book – what you liked or disliked about the characters, scenes or messages.

4 Read an online review of *The Humans*. Complete the review with the words in the box.

> absolutely   alien   comfortable
> main   professor

REVIEW

The Humans
by Matt Haig

I've just read a really funny novel called *The Humans*. It was written by English author Matt Haig. The ¹_____ character is an ²_____ who finds himself in the body of a dead university ³_____. The alien is sent to Earth to destroy evidence that the professor had solved a big mathematical problem, but the alien soon finds himself learning more about the professor, his family and 'the humans' than he ever expected. When he becomes ⁴_____ living with his family, who have no idea he's not the real Andrew, the alien must choose between returning home or finding a new home here on Earth. I ⁵_____ loved it!

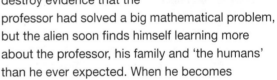

5 You are going to write an online book review. Think about a book that you like and plan your review. Use the notes to help you.

- What is the title of the book?
- Who is the author?
- Who is the main character?
- What happens in the story?
- What is your opinion of it?

6 Write your online book review.

- Write about 100 words.
- Remember to check your spelling and grammar.

VOCABULARY Collocations: thinking

1 Put the letters in the correct order to make thinking collocations.

1 keam pu uroy dimn ....
2 seu yoru migantoinia ....
3 rcsos yuro dimn ....
4 evah a ohtuhtg ....
5 veha osecnd tugohtsh ....
6 vieg sonemoe a thin ....
7 eosl yuro ticoenanocrtn ....

2 Complete the sentences with the correct collocations from Exercise 1.

1 If you suddenly start thinking about something, you ....
2 To help them to guess something, you can ....
3 When people are talking in an exam, you can ....
4 When you are an artist, you have to ....
5 When you have an important decision to make, it's hard to ....
6 Sometimes you can .... about something and decide not to do it.
7 If you think about something for a short time, it ....

3 Choose the correct collocation.

1 Shall I go out tonight? I can't *make up my mind / cross my mind*.
2 My sister was playing her music too loud when I was doing my homework. I *had second thoughts / lost my concentration*.
3 I wanted Jemma to guess what her present was – so I *had a thought / gave her a hint*.
4 What was the first thing that *gave you a hint / crossed your mind* when you won the prize?
5 I was going to play football on Saturday, but I *lost my concentration / had second thoughts* and went to the cinema instead.
6 I had to write a story for homework, so I *used my imagination / made up my mind* to create the characters.
7 Have you found anyone to play guitar in the band yet? If not, I've just *had a thought / given you a hint*.

4 Choose the correct form of the collocations from Exercise 1 to complete the text.

Before the maths exam yesterday, it [1] .... that I might not pass it. There was one really difficult question in the exam where I couldn't [2] .... what the answer was. And to make it worse, there were some students behind me, talking all the time, so I [3] .... All I really wanted was for someone to [4] .... so I could answer the question, but obviously that doesn't happen in an exam. So instead, I just started dreaming and tried to [5] .... After the exam finished, I [6] .... that I might not continue with the subject next year. But then I [7] .... and decided that it was best to continue.

$3x^2 - 2xy$

$e = \sum_{n=0}^{\infty} \frac{1}{n!}$

$x = \frac{-b \pm \sqrt{b^2 - 4ac}}{2a}$

$ax^2 + bx + c = 0$

$x = \frac{S}{P}$

$E = mc^2$

READING

1 Look at the picture. What can you see? Do you think everything in the picture is real? What do you think is real or not real?

2 Read the article quickly. How does Julian Beever create his art?

3 Read the article again. Are these sentences true (T) or false (F)?

1 Julian created pavement art using paint.
2 When people walk past his art on the street, they believe what they see is real.
3 From the start, he's always thinking about how his creation will look in a photograph.
4 Beever's time is mostly spent trying to get the best position in the street.
5 Beever thinks the internet is a great way for people to see his art.
6 He also spends a lot of time recreating the work of very famous artists.

4 Match the highlighted words in the text to their meanings.

1 people who have complete knowledge or skill in something
2 the direction from which you look at something
3 pictures of people
4 square pieces of hard material, such as stone or metal, used to cover walls and floor
5 a place to walk on the side of a road

Julian Beever started creating pavement art while he was attending art school. He made two-dimensional drawings using chalk (something teachers use to write on blackboards) and people gave him money. He began experimenting with chalk creations after seeing tiles being removed from a street, an effect he tried to recreate on paper.

When looked at in a photograph, Beever's creations look amazingly realistic. Those who walk past them don't get quite the same view, though. The 3-D (three-dimensional) optical illusion effect works only from one particular angle: the place where Beever positions his camera. From any other angle, the work looks strange.

For Beever, the pavement creation isn't the end result. He explains, 'For me, I'm working towards building a photograph as my end result.' This means a lot of his time is used running between the camera and the drawing, making sure each line is in just the right place to create the 3-D look.

While some artists might feel it would be a waste of time to create art that can be seen from only one angle – and that is usually damaged within a few days – Beever doesn't mind, and he sees the internet as the best way to show his art. Without the internet, his work wouldn't really be known. But with the internet, his work never really disappears and it's seen by a lot more people than if it was in a museum.

Beever studied at an art school and he can recreate the art of the masters as well as paint formal portraits. However, most of his time and energy is used for the 3-D pavement art which has made him famous. He believes his art allows everyone to look at and enjoy art: 'My art is for anybody. It's for people who wouldn't go into an art gallery. It's art for the people.'

1 Write full sentences, using the past simple passive.

1 The first / Ames room / construct / Adelbert Ames Jr

2 It / build / 1946

3 An Ames room / create / for / the film star's / latest / film

4 The actor / tell / not / to move

5 This trick / use / many / films

6 My photo / take / Ames room / museum / San Francisco

2 Choose the correct verb form.

1 The race *was won* / *is won* by an Olympic runner.
2 Every night, the news on TV *is read* / *are read* by the same lady.
3 The artists *were paid* / *are paid* to draw 3-D pictures on the wall of the shop.
4 My dad *was asked* / *is asked* to talk to the school about his job.
5 Every year, the poster for the music festival *are designed* / *is designed* by the school.
6 The illusion *was created* / *is created* to make people think in a different way.
7 That exercise *was done* / *is done* last week in class.
8 The adverts *was made* / *were made* in our studio in London.

3 Complete the second sentence so that it means the same as the first.

1 My grandfather built the house 50 years ago.
The house _____ my grandfather 50 years ago.
2 Someone delivers our post every day.
Our post _____ every day.
3 Our teacher showed us the illusion.
We _____ our teacher.
4 My friend did this painting.
This painting _____ my friend.
5 The film used a lot of 3-D graphics.
A lot of 3-D _____ in the film.
6 That place designed interesting clothes.
Interesting clothes _____ at that place.
7 Our team won the game.
The game _____ our team.
8 The magician made the rabbit disappear.
The rabbit _____ by the magician.

4 Complete the text with the past simple passive form of the verbs in the box.

base	call	direct	film
show	tell	write	

FILM REVIEW

A film [1] _____ in our local cinema last week. It [2] _____ *The Illusionist*. It [3] _____ by Neil Burger. The story [4] _____ on a short story called *Eisenhem the Illusionist*. This story [5] _____ by Steven Millhauser. My friend and I [6] _____ the story by our teacher. According to one website, the story takes place in Austria, but actually it [7] _____ in the Czech Republic.

5 Choose the correct sentence in each pair.

1 a We have been making optical illusions together since we were borned.
  b We have been making optical illusions together since we were born.
2 a It was my 15th birthday party, and the place where the party was organised was in a park.
  b It was my 15th birthday party, and the place where was organised the party was in a park.
3 a A street in Tokyo was covered in 3-D art.
  b A street in Tokyo were covered in 3-D art.
4 a He looked shy, but then I got to know him better and were surprised by all the things we had in common.
  b He looked shy, but then I got to know him better and was surprised by all the things we had in common.
5 a The first city that we visited was called Vielle.
  b The first city that we visited we call Vielle.

VOCABULARY   *look (at), see, watch*

1 Choose the correct verb to complete the sentences.

1 *Look at / See* that cat. It's a very unusual colour!
2 I've had second thoughts. I will *look at / watch* *Game of Thrones* instead of *Hunger Games*.
3 I can't *watch / see* the illusion in the picture! Can you give me a hint?
4 I lose my concentration very easily, so I try not to *see / look at* the clock when I'm doing my homework!
5 On Saturdays, I always *look at / watch* my favourite football team.
6 I can't wait to *see / watch* all my friends at the party this weekend!
7 When I wear my glasses, I can *watch / see* much better.
8 I need to catch the bus to work, so I will *look at / watch* the timetable.

2 Choose the correct verb to complete the sentences.

1 I love to *look at / see / watch* my favourite basketball team on Tuesdays.
2 It crossed my mind last night that I didn't *look at / see / watch* Sabrina at the party.
3 Are you *looking at / seeing / watching* that new series that everyone is talking about on Channel 7?
4 *Look at / See / Watch* that street art. It's amazing!
5 Have you *looked at / seen / watched* the new Star Wars film at the cinema yet?
6 They are hiding. They don't want anyone to *look at / see / watch* them.
7 Please *look at / see / watch* the examples in the book and write your own sentences.
8 I had to use my imagination to *look at / see / watch* the illusion in the picture.

3 Complete the sentences using the correct form of *look at*, *see* or *watch*. Sometimes there is more than one correct answer.

1 I _____ a great film last night!
2 I _____ my watch and decided it was time for some lunch.
3 Richard said he _____ a famous person in London, but he wouldn't tell me who!
4 The final of the Eurovision Song Contest was _____ by over 180 million people this year.
5 I was _____ the match when the phone rang.
6 I love _____ my friends after school.
7 I don't know why he was _____ me like that.

LISTENING

🔊 **1** You will hear an interview with a young magician called Jerry Tweed. Tick the topics you think he will talk about. Then listen and check.

1 how he became interested in doing magic ☐
2 how he started learning tricks ☐
3 how much money he's made doing magic ☐
4 his favourite trick to perform ☐
5 what his parents think about him doing magic ☐
6 what he would like do in the future ☐

🔊 **2** Listen again. For each question, choose the correct answer A, B or C.

1 Who first encouraged Jerry to start doing magic tricks?
   A his aunt
   B a performer
   C his father
2 Jerry learned his first magic tricks when he
   A watched a teacher at school.
   B had some private lessons.
   C joined a special club.
3 What does Jerry do now to develop his skills?
   A He goes to see other magicians perform.
   B He reads books about how to do magic.
   C He finds videos online showing tricks.
4 How do Jerry's parents feel about him leaving school early?
   A They believe he has the ability to have a good career.
   B They are happy to give him money when he needs it.
   C They would still like him to take all his exams.
5 How does Jerry feel about his appearance on television?
   A surprised by the way the presenter reacted
   B unsure whether some tricks he did were original enough
   C pleased at the number of people who watched the programme
6 What is Jerry definitely going to do in the future?
   A train people in his own school
   B travel to other countries for work
   C design magic equipment for learners

Acknowledgements

The authors and publishers acknowledge the following sources of copyright material and are grateful for the permissions granted. While every effort has been made, it has not always been possible to identify the sources of all the material used, or to trace all copyright holders. If any omissions are brought to our notice, we will be happy to include the appropriate acknowledgements on reprinting and in the next update to the digital edition, as applicable.

Key: U = Unit.

Text

U18: Text adapted from 'How To Find Your Dream Job' by Brian Tracy, https://www.briantracy.com/blog/business-success/steps-on-how-to-find-your-dream-job/ . Copyright © Brian Tracy International. Reproduced with kind permission; **U20:** Text adapted from 'Chalk It Up To Imagination: Julian Beever' by Andréa Fernandes, 28.07.2008. Copyright © Mental Floss. Reproduced with permission.

Photography
The following images are sourced from Getty Images.

U1: jarenwicklund/iStock/Getty Images Plus; **U2:** Halfpoint/iStock/Getty Images Plus; Matias Castello/EyeEm; kali9/E+; **U3:** Wavebreak Media Ltd/Getty Images Plus; **U4:** SolStock/E+; Syldavia/iStock/Getty Images Plus; fstop123/Getty Images Plus; yulkapopkova/Vetta; XiXinXing; Ababsolutum/iStock/Getty Images Plus; Luigi Masella/EyeEm; **U5:** jacoblund/iStock/Getty Images Plus; Peter Dazeley/Photographer's Choice; Bill Hinton/Moment; MachineHeadz/iStock/Getty Images Plus; Andrew Bret Wallis/Photographer's Choice RF; Image Source; South_agency/E+; Daria Botieva/Eyeem; Jaromir Chalabala/EyeEm; **U6:** AndreaAstes/iStock Editorial/Getty Images Plus; Tanya Ann Photography/Moment; Catherine Ledner/The Image Bank; **U7:** Westend61; **U8:** PeopleImages/E+; Kathleen Finlay/Image Source; Bernard Tan/EyeE; John Lund/Marc Romanelli/Blend Images; **U9:** Jupiterimages/Stockbyte; Bloom Productions/Taxi; Martin Barraud/OJO Images; Jaap Arriens/NurPhoto; **U10:** Paul Beinssen/Lonely Planet Images; BRETT STEVENS/Cultura; **U11:** Drazen_/E+; blue jean images; **U12:** taviphoto/iStock/Getty Images Plus; Danita Delimont/Gallo Images; Samuli Vainionpää/Moment; tenra/iStock/Getty Images Plus; Andra Junaidi/EyeEm; TORSTEN BLACKWOOD/AFP; Tom Kelley Archive/Retrofile RF; vgajic/E+; **U14:** mbbirdy/E+; Jon Kopaloff/FilmMagic; Caspar Benson; **U15:** Westend61; **U16:** archives/E+; Thomas-Soellner/iStock/Getty Images Plus; Ryan McVay/Photodisc; nata_zhekova/iStock/Getty Images Plus; esseffe/iStock/Getty Images Plus; Monty Rakusen/Cultura; **U17:** Neilson Barnard/Getty Images Entertainment; Hemera Technologies/AbleStock.com/Getty Images Plus; Vera Anderson/WireImage; **U18:** warrengoldswain/iStock/Getty Images Plus; Flashpop/Stone; bowdenimages/iStock/Getty Images Plus; **U19:** Philippe TURPIN/Photononsto; **U20:** Westend61; paul mansfield photography/Moment.

The following photographs have been sourced from other library/sources.

U19: Courtesy of Canongate Books Ltd.; Copyright © 2011 by Veronica Roth. Used by permission of HarperCollins Publishers. **U20:** © Julian Beever; Snap Stills/Rex.

Front cover photography by oxygen/Moment/Getty Images.

Illustration
Chris Chalik (The Bright Agency); Ludovic Salle (Advocate Art); Stuart Harrison; Alek Sotirovski (Beehive Illustration).

URLS
The publisher has made every effort to ensure that the URLs for external websites referred to in this book are correct and active at the time of printing. However, the publisher takes no responsibility for the websites and can make no guarantees that sites will remain live or that their content is or will remain appropriate.

The publishers are grateful to the following contributors: author of *Cambridge English Prepare! First Edition* Level 4 Workbook: Niki Joseph; cover design and design concept: restless; typesetting: emc design Ltd; audio recordings: produced by Leon Chambers and recorded at The SoundHouse Studios, London